ARCHITECTURAL DESIGN

EDITORIAL OFFICES:
42 LEINSTER GARDENS, LONDON W2 3AN
TEL: 0171-402 2141 FAX: 0171-723 9540

EDITOR: Maggie Toy
EDITORIAL TEAM: Iona Baird, Stephen Watt, Jane Richards
ART EDITOR: Andrea Bettella
CHIEF DESIGNER: Mario Bettella
DESIGNERS: Alex Young, Alistair Probert

CONSULTANTS: Catherine Cooke, Terry Farrell, Kenneth Frampton, Charles Jencks, Heinrich Klotz, Leon Krier, Robert Maxwell, Demetri Porphyrios, Kenneth Powell, Colin Rowe, Derek Walker

SUBSCRIPTION OFFICES:
UK: ACADEMY GROUP LTD
42 LEINSTER GARDENS
LONDON W2 3AN
TEL: 0171-402 2141 FAX: 0171-723 9540

USA AND CANADA: VCH PUBLISHERS NEW YORK INC, SUITE 907, 220 EAST 23RD STREET NEW YORK, NY 10010-4606
TEL: (212) 683 8333 FAX: (212) 779 8890

ALL OTHER COUNTRIES:
VCH VERLAGSGESELLSCHAFT MBH
BOSCHSTRASSE 12, POSTFACH 101161
69451 WEINHEIM
FEDERAL REPUBLIC OF GERMANY
TEL: +49 6201 606 148 FAX: +49 6201 606 184

Architectural Design is published six times per year (Jan/Feb; Mar/Apr; May/Jun; Jul/Aug; Sept/Oct; and Nov/Dec). Subscription rates for 1996 (incl p&p): Annual subscription price: UK only £68.00, World DM 195, USA $142.00 for regular subscribers. Student rate: UK only £50.00, World DM 156, USA $105.00 incl postage and handling charges. Individual issues: £16.95/DM 42.50 (plus £2.40/DM 6 for p&p, per issue ordered), US $28.95 (incl p&p).
For the USA and Canada, Architectural Design is distributed by VCH Publishers New York Inc, Suite 907, 220 East 23rd Street New York, NY 10010-4606; Tel: (212) 683 8333, Fax: (212) 779 8890. Application to mail at second-class postage rates is pending at New York, NY. POSTMASTER. Send address changes to Architectural Design, VCH Publishers New York Inc, Suite 907, 220 East 23rd Street, New York, NY 10010-4606. Printed in Italy. Origination by Media 2000, London.
All prices are subject to change without notice. [ISSN: 0003-8504]

CONTENTS

Analysis carried out at the Zaanstad workshops using the Space Syntax tool

Spiller Farmer Architects, 'Landscape Matters', exhibition design, Building Centre, London

Studio 333, Prado Museum Extension, model

BATTLE McCARTHY
MULTI-SOURCE SYNTHESIS
Dynamic Cities

The nature of our cities and towns defines the qualities of civilisation itself. Yet at present their development is a stilted and haphazard process of change, responding to the skewed objectives of individual pressures rather than the functional organic growth of the whole.

We separate the producer from the consumer, the farmer from the kitchen, the power plant from the appliance, the dump site from the garbage can, the banker from the borrower and depositor, and inevitably, the government from the citizenry. Development becomes a process by which we separate authority and responsibility, where those who make decisions are not affected by the decisions.

Morris, quoted in *Reviving the City*
There are two challenges for the design and management of cities in the 21st century. First, the functions and operation of urban areas must be better understood, so that cities can work at maximum efficiency. Second, the process of design and decision-making must be developed to address a broad base of constituencies and needs: social, economic and environmental.

The form of cities has always been driven by the interaction of certain critical forces: the market, or the need to trade; patterns and technologies of movement; the distribution and availability of energy; the supply and distribution of water; the safe and effective disposal of waste, and the availability of natural resources. A number of analysis tools are currently being evolved which will help people to consider all of these elements as part of the public discussion to shape the development of cities. This progress is contemporaneous with the application of participative design, which ensures that the widest range of issues are considered during the design process, and that when proposals do emerge, they can proceed with the support and contributions of the citizens.

Battle McCarthy have recently taken part in such a process in the town of Zaanstad, on the northern periphery of Amsterdam. The chief planner, Miranda Reitsma, was asked to prepare a set of proposals for a problematic and undeveloped area to the west of the town centre. Unwilling to tackle such a difficult site with conventional planning techniques, she invited Chris Moller of Studio 333 to help set up a new process based on design workshops. The objective was to create a resilient and flexible framework for future development on the site and discover the catalysts of infrastructure required to set it in motion. The workshops were organised around three themes, recognised early on as critical for the success of any proposals to the site: movement; landscape and ecology, and diversification of use.

A range of people, from within the local authority and external consultancies, were invited to join the process. At each workshop, traffic engineers, landscape ecologists and building and urban designers were invited to describe their own objectives for the area, and to participate in explorations of the range of potential solutions.

The organisers set out to make a range of tools available to the workshop groups so that each issue could be properly investigated and understood. Working with two postgraduate groups from the Bartlett School of Architecture, University College London, the participants were able to apply two relevant computer programs: Space Syntax, to understand movement, and Pangea, a 3D sketch design tool used here to investigate building density and use.

The following pages illustrate and describe the analysis carried out in the workshops, and the outline proposals arising from the work, presented under a series of headings. 'Movement', 'Urban Mix', 'Ecology and Water', and 'Synthesis'. The process is still ongoing, and it is hoped that further tools will be developed and applied as the design progresses.

Information on Space Syntax and Pangea is available on the internet at the following addresses:

http://doric.bart.ucl.ac.uk/web/slab/slabhome.html
http://doric.bart.ucl.ac.uk/web/Pangea/
Intelligent Architecture

The Intelligent Architecture project is funded by DTi and EPSRC. Funding collaborators on the project are: Avanti Architects Ltd, Bovis Construction Ltd, Broadgate Properties Ltd, Criterion Software Ltd, DEGW London Ltd, Oscar Faber Consultant Ltd, PowerGen PLC, Richard Rogers Partnership, Small-World Systems Ltd, Qualum Ltd, UCL Bartlett and UCL Computer Science.

OPPOSITE: The East End of London drawn by Booth in the 1890s; INSERTS, FROM ABOVE: Movement; urban mix; built form; synthesis; FROM ABOVE: Site analysis; typical view of wetlands to the west

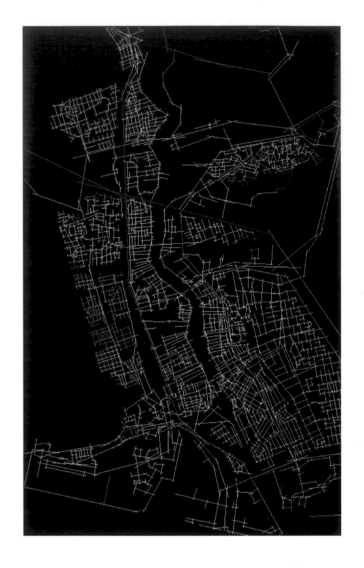

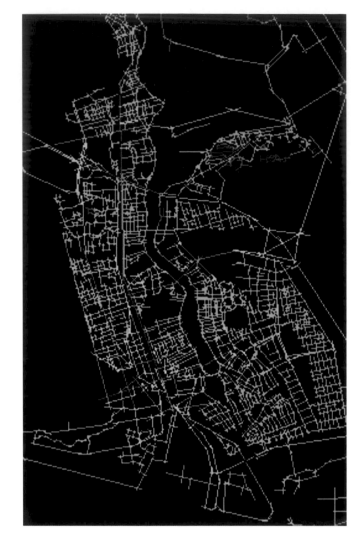

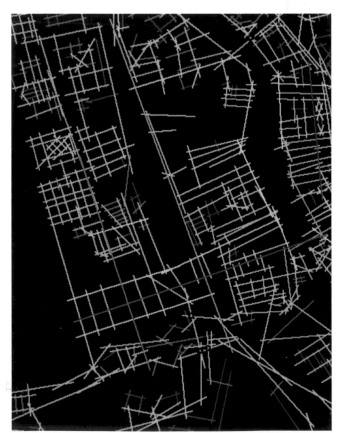

Analysis carried out at the workshops, using the Space Syntax tool, was critical to the design group's understanding of the site.

FROM ABOVE, LEFT TO RIGHT: Axial map of Zaanstad showing global integration. The road and railway line at the centre of the town create a clear break between the east and west sides; Early model of the site with sketch proposal developed at the workshop. Routes are created across the railway increasing the integration of the west side; Extending the existing high street across the railway, to the west extends the 'strip effect'. As more connections are established, a locally intelligible district begins to emerge.

Zaanstad
MOVEMENT

Movement is central to the operation and shape of cities. As Jane Jacobs pointed out, it is likely that urbanisation itself developed as a result of movement through trade, as early man began to realise that a resource which was plentiful and cheap in one location could be rare and valuable somewhere else. The most successful early conurbations were those located at the crossing of trade routes, places where people could interact and barter. The primary purpose of cities, and what makes them dynamic places, is essentially the same, and the heart of a successful city is a bustling street.

There are many theories of how people move through cities. The controversial theorist Kevin Lynch has argued that urban navigation and movement is guided by visual and cultural landmarks. There is also a common assumption that key activities can be located relatively independently of spatial patterns. However, the research of Professor Bill Hillier, and others at the Bartlett, has demonstrated that layout is at least as important in directing movement as any other factor. They have also developed a mathematical modelling tool, Space Syntax, to calculate the 'integration' of each space within a city; the accessibility of each space from every other space in the system. Studies have shown a strong relationship between integration and levels of movement in urban areas.

The analysis has the advantage that it is immediate and visual – categorising well integrated spaces as warm, or red, and the least integrated spaces as cool, or blue – and is ideal for participative design. At Zaanstad it was possible to test different proposals for the town and site in a very short time. Each graphic model is supported by a statistical database, which allows users to pick out new lines of movement, within a scattergram of the whole, and examine its spatial properties in detail.

The design proposals, based on this analysis, involve extending the existing shopping street across the railway to the west, enhancing its 'strip effect' as a strong, well-integrated space. The railway station at the centre of this route provides excellent connections to the centre of Amsterdam and the surrounding region. The extended space forms a spine to the new development, and secondary streets begin to define the likely building massing.

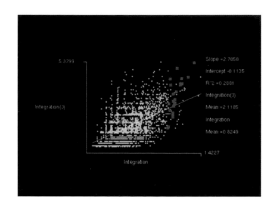

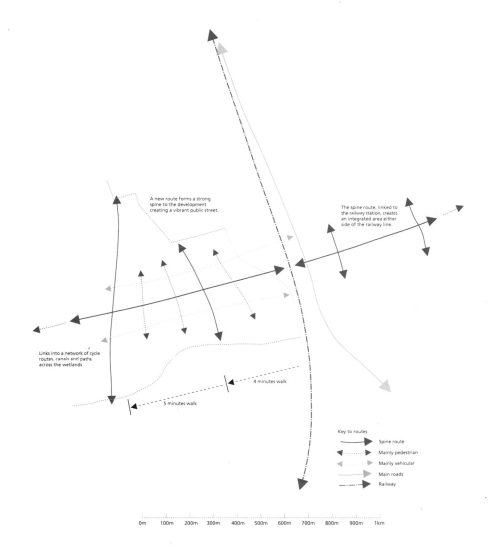

FROM ABOVE, LEFT TO RIGHT: Aerial view of Oxford Street in central London, an example of a strong route; Scattergram of the Zaanstad proposal, with key routes highlighted in red, illustrating the effect of a strong central route; Movement strategy proposed for the site

Zaanstad
URBAN MIX

Cities are shaped by what people do in them. Each activity has implications for the types of building and spaces, and the people who occupy them. The diversity of activities is critical, affecting value and hence development quality, social mix, population densities and levels of crime, as well as many issues to do with infrastructure sizing, cost and sustainability.

For Zaanstad, a sketch design tool was required which would allow people to investigate possible arrangements of building types and begin to understand how this affects the quality of development and sustainability. This can be carried out with a spreadsheet program, but this would be of only limited usefulness without the limitations of a site and an understanding of the urban consequences.

The Intelligent Architecture project at the Bartlett has been developing software which allows a 3D modelling and viewing program to link into a range of other applications. The program, Pangea, provides a powerful basic tool for a huge range of possible applications, and aims to enable an integrated platform for tasks from design to management.

Pangea's advantage is its robustness and simplicity. Its user interface is direct and intuitive, avoiding the complications of CAD, so that anyone can use it. It allows the participants to sketch in 3D, alter and tweak objects and move around in the environment created. Each object has the potential for simple intelligence.

The simple model developed for the first stage of the exercise was informed by the relationship between movement and building densities. Every building is modelled as a 3D object which knows its designated use and floor area. This is linked to a speadsheet which works out the expected daily and annual profiles for population, electricity and heating. As the user explores the development, the user can select blocks, change use, size or height, and observe how this changes the spreadsheet graphs. The program also colours the model to provide a direct visual interpretation of energy demand and occupation over time.

The designers intend to extend the model, to include land values and rental, so that a social charter can be established. Once an acceptable diversity of occupation and activity is achieved, it will be possible to demonstrate, for example, how higher value development can be used to balance the cost of social housing and maintain a high quality of public space.

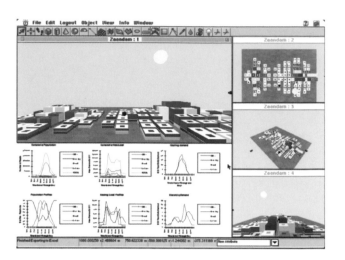

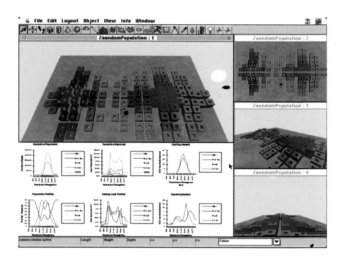

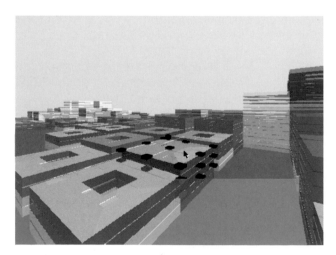

Pangea screen views Zaanstad. The user can walk around the model and change the use and size of blocks, while the daily energy demand, movement and population profiles are plotted on a series of graphs. The objective of achieving a good mix of uses is to even out load profiles.

Zaanstad
WATER AND ECOLOGY

Any process of urbanisation affects the surrounding landscape and wildlife. The task of careful design is to minimise such impact, and to create ecological niches where they did not exist before. The Zaanstad site is partially developed and has little wildlife or ecological value. However, the wetlands to the west are an area of regional importance, providing a habitat for migrant species of bird and a wide range of insects. It was a priority that the national value of the site should provide a special character for the development.

The wetlands themselves are reclaimed land, being used historically for dairy and sheep farming, and it is this combination of activities which has created its unique ecology. Unfortunately, farming is no longer profitable on the land, which is increasingly under-used. It is the objective of the Zaanstad development to instigate an increased, but carefully managed, level of public access to the wetlands, maintaining the momentum and investment required to protect the area.

Areas appropriate for the preservation of wildlife are in many ways described by an inverse of the movement analysis; where people do not go, nature is undisturbed. The effect of the proposed infrastructure would be to make it possible to create an ecological corridor into the town from the wetlands, a transitional zone from urban park to nature.

The water of the wetlands is slightly brackish, a rare quality contributing to its ecological value. Therefore the control of pollution is essential. As well as a system of recycling 'grey water' in buildings to reduce consumption, the designers have proposed the use of biologically based water treatment systems, integrated with the landscape immediately surrounding the new buildings, to purify surface water from roofs and streets before it is allowed to enter the wetlands. This zone of ponds, reed beds and marshes forms a buffer between the wetlands and the development, both physically and visually.

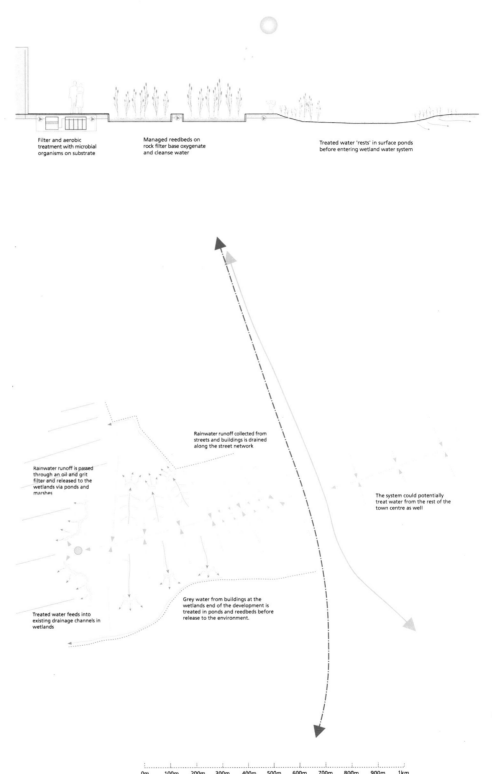

FROM ABOVE: Proposed surface water treatment system; proposed surface water strategy

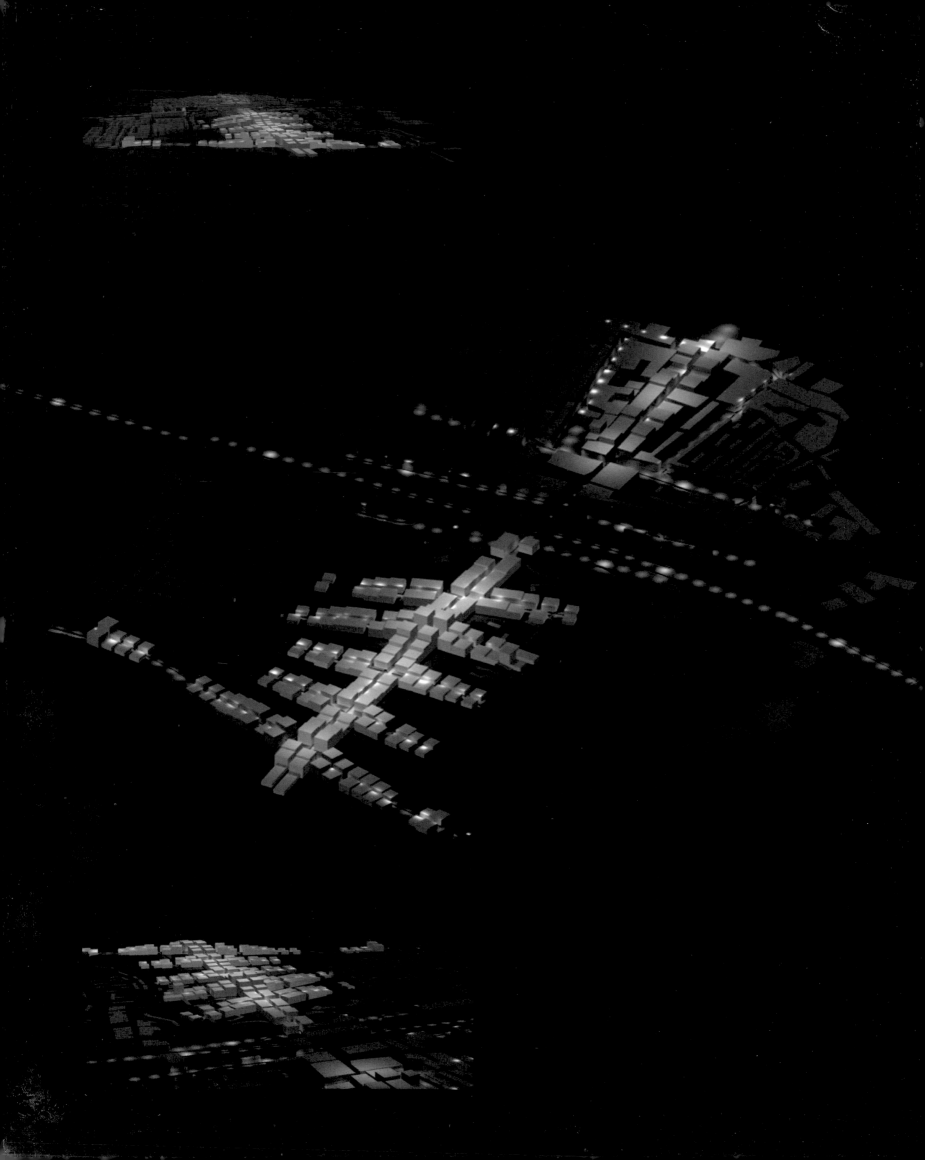

Zaanstad
SYNTHESIS

The process and the tools used here demonstrate some basic principles with the potential for future development. At the heart of this approach is a belief that a firm understanding of functional and engineering principles can lead to the development of rational and successful form. Ensuring a robust strategy for fundamental issues such as movement and energy makes the city work better and increases its sustainability, allowing form and quality to arise directly from specific local conditions. Bringing engineering and design disciplines together can overcome specialist disputes and create a coherent intent. It can reduce infrastructure costs, minimise environmental impact and help ensure a multifaceted design solution whose complexity reflects that of reality.

At Zaanstad, the generation of the proposals is a response to the nature of the site. Movement and ecology have encountered each other and tried to reach an equilibrium. This has suggested form.

Perhaps the most important principle is that the city is for people. Maintaining a vibrant urban environment and public realm is critical to the health of civilisation. There is a need for design tools and processes which allow people to participate in decision-making, to understand the engineering issues involved, and to sketch creatively and observe the implications of different options. Tools such as Pangea and Space Syntax are the first generation of these. But this approach also offers the opportunity for a wider social and economic vision to be developed.

Past attempts to consider social policy as part of design have been hindered by distant and clumsy bureaucracies. Designers have now realised that a higher level of individual empowerment and participation is required, but many present political systems seem biased against this. At Zaanstad, the design group hopes to establish a framework which will enable a variety of individual and partisan objectives to be satisfied within a whole that is greater than its parts.

The authors would like to thank: Robert Webb, Andrew Grant and Wyn Davies from Battle McCarthy; Tim Stonor and Mark David Major from the Space Syntax Laboratory at the Bartlett, UCL; and Alan Penn and Ruth Conroy from the Intelligent Architecture project at the Bartlett, UCL.

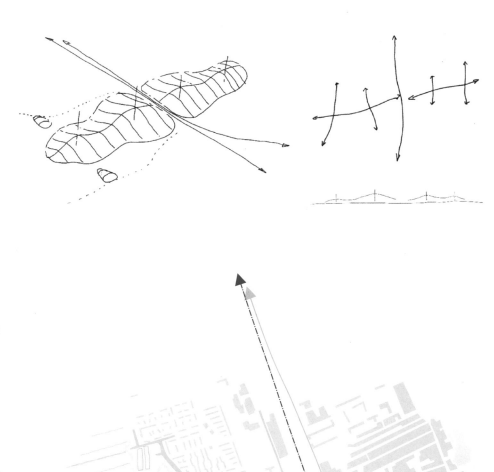

0m   100m   200m   300m   400m   500m   600m   700m   800m   900m   1km

OPPOSITE: Potential massing; FROM ABOVE: Massing model; Development zones shaped by movement and landscape

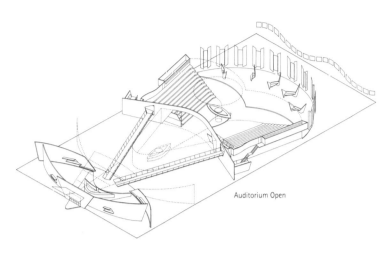

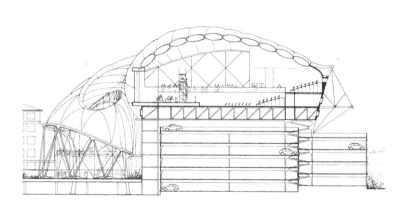

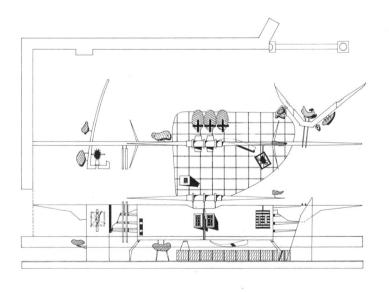

ABOVE: Apicella Associates, ICL computer environment, exhibition design, Birmingham; CENTRE: Birds Portchmouth Russum, Fairfield Culture Dome, Croydon; BELOW: Spiller Farmer Architects, 'Landscape Matters', exhibition design, London

KESTER RATTENBURY
YOUNG ARCHITECTS

The 'baby boom' generation have always seemed unwilling to relinquish their youth; continuing to live like students in an attempt to postpone the normal process of settling down into a productive middle age. The 80s youth vogue (formalised in the 90s by the great infantilisation marketing campaigns) is a difficult habit for the individual to kick, and perhaps unsurprisingly, it seems to have a professional knock-on effect. When the word about this issue went out around London, there was a certain clutch of usual suspects who inevitably expected to be involved: they have built buildings; they are running practices, and they are 'young architects'. Indeed, they have been young architects for so long that the meaning of the term, like modernism, has become semi-detached from its usage.

This is partly because these practices have earned their status, as the new architectural establishment, by virtue of a combination of their personal youth and espousal of a new modernism. This version is flexible, soft, intelligent and not particularly political, or at least reflects a loss of faith with pro-active political agendas and grand plans: which is partly connected to the belief in a smaller scale, a local or individual ideal, and partly compromised by their dependent position on the tail-end of the 80s free market; the constant political dilemma of architectural idealism. In any case, the architectural crusade of this era was different; it was to win permission for the continuing development of modernity itself.

Ten years before Prince Charles got onto it, the British architectural profession was dealing with its own crisis of confidence. After the great post-war housing estates fell into disrepair and disrepute in the 70s, large-scale architectural Utopianism was firmly out of favour, and the puzzled, guilty and idealistic moved first into the realms of neo-vernacular and romantic pragmatism and community involvement. But in the usual time lag between buildings and ideas, this was the first stage of a re-emerging confidence, supported by the building boom which overtook it and produced, *inter alia*, the undoubtedly great expressions of the high-tech, Lloyd's and the Hongkong and Shanghai Bank. First via Rogers and Foster, and later through a generation of smaller practices, who were occasionally able to find some commissions, a new guerrilla campaign on a suspicious, but interested, public was up and running, proposing the idea of a new and likeable modernism.

However, it was not just the second-generation Fosters and Rogers – the Future Systems, Richard Hordens and Chris Wilkinsons – who were significant players in this. The battle was largely taken up by an archipelago of young, important, small, intelligent and friendly practices, for whom there is currently no generic term. Their work is rooted in the forms and ideals of modernism, but it also brings in carefully retrieved elements of classical phrasing, abstract expressionism, neo-vernacular softening and the adoption of current artistic techniques and technical innovations, and has connections with the ideas and expressions of deconstructivism, or even post-modernism, but it does not look much like them. It operates somewhere between the extraordinary formal refinements of the ordinary by Foster and the glorious picturesque expressions of the necessary by Rogers; between Cullinan's use of modernist and arts and crafts techniques and manners in the service of a community ideal and the 80s consumer boom with its cult object fetishes. Like the smaller works of modernism, it develops this with a specific and intellectual precision. It is often undoubtedly and overwhelmingly charming and cunning. Expressly intelligent, it maintains a direct intellectual feed with academia, which supports the emergence of small practices, and a visible sense of public conscience. But it is also inherently related to the commercial consumerist world which produced it, expressed through its object fetishism and inevitable desire to please the client. It is high-quality, intelligent architecture which, because of its contemporary and historical context, keeps its polemic wryly tucked into the pursuit of being liked.

This is a very British situation, re-negotiating a passage for the new, in the aftermath of Prince Charles' reification of a driving nostalgia and the flagrantly modern 80s building boom, by a culture predisposed to the new, yet with a profound suspicion of newness. The same period in France was marked by an assumption of political and public will in favour of the new

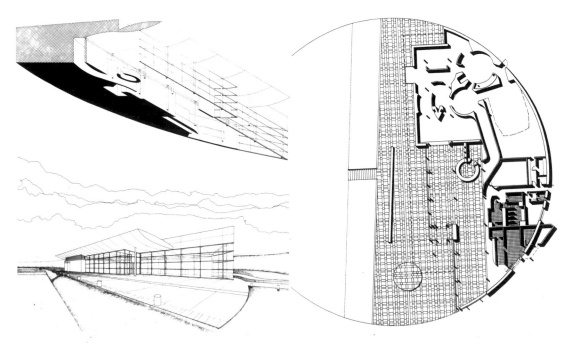

ABOVE LEFT: Alford Hall Monaghan Morris Architects, Live-in Room House, exhibition project; ABOVE RIGHT: Sauerbruch Hutton, Heinrich Heine Strasse, Berlin; CENTRE, LEFT: Studio Granda, Eva fashion shop, Reykjavik; CENTRE RIGHT: Richard Murphy Architects, restaurant, Inverewe Gardens, Wester Ross; BELOW: Allan Murray Associates, Peterhead Maritime Heritage Centre

and dramatic, incorporating a system designed to support this. Now that the state building programme is declining, French architects are facing their own confidence crisis, being unsure how well equipped they are to deal with the uncertain economics of competing internationally. Alternatively, in Vienna and Los Angeles expressive polemicism was all the rage, while Japan remained traditionally in search of the new, and in Italy it is still difficult for practices to get published unless they have connections with the often self-owned publishing houses.

Britain remained engaged but distinct from these influences, as it was in the throes of its own very significant zone of cultural transition. This generation has, of course, been able to operate with strong support from its own modern history – particularly modernism and Archigram – while appearing radical to a public who are still fairly unfamiliar with architecture. The innovations of this generation have included a female softening of the high-tech toys for boys into smaller domestic or commercial fields. At the same time those influences which are alleged to be shaping the next generation have been firmly identified; the influence of cinema, advertising and electronic communications. Again, these are inherent to the legacy of Archigram, and yet surprisingly it is now that they are becoming integrated into everyday society.

It would be possible to say that there is evidence here both of idealism and disingenuity. In modernism there is perhaps more delicate irony, and less manifest cynicism, than in some of the expressions of the newer generation – what David Greene calls 'buy-me-believe-in-me' – though indeed, the intentions are akin; both maintain the notion of idealism, yet choose to express it differently. In comparison to modernism, however, the work of this generation has strongly mixed the notion of Utopia with the concept of politically dependent impotence. In our recent era, Baucis and Philemon's ideal cottage has not only been set up in opposition to, but is also ambiguously dependent on, the Faustian developer.

In publications like these, one is constantly tempted to extrapolate ideas from small buildings; a very dangerous but interesting pastime. Media like this cannot present the buildings themselves, only pictures and writing about them. Yet it is through these actual buildings that the practices have enacted their role as ambassadors for the new to a suspicious public, and they have done it very well. In default of Charles Jencks coming up with another name for them, they should be allowed to keep their title of 'Young Architects'; they have earned it.

Carlos Villanueva Brandt, Shogawa Pavilion, Japan

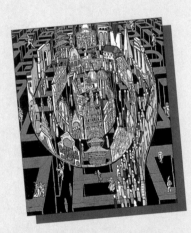

NANCY WOLF
HIDDEN CITIES, HIDDEN LONGINGS

Karen A Franck

In the latest Art & Design Monograph, American artist Nancy Wolf leads the reader through her life and art; from the earliest work, when she first began commenting on architecture and society, to the most recent drawings, which pose compelling alternatives to the anonymous modern cityscape. Wolf vividly portrays the coldness and sterility of modernism, the superficiality of post-modernism, and the possibilities for change in deconstructivism. She has integrated her pointed critiques of these architectural movements with her own experiences of alienation in an urban renewal area in Washington, DC, the devastation of New York in the 70s and 80s, and the warmth and intimacy of traditional communities in Africa and Asia.

Wolf's message is clear: contemporary western architecture and planning have lost sight of people; cities, buildings and public spaces leave inhabitants disconnected from each other and from the places where they live and work.

A foreword by Peter Blake, an introduction by Karen A Franck, and a lively, informal dialogue between her and Nancy Wolf frame the spectacular images. At times the tone is sombre, but there is always a sense of hope for a different kind of architecture; one that embraces people and celebrates community.

A retrospective exhibition of Nancy Wolf's work, 'Architecture Revealed', is to be shown at the American Institute of Architects in Washington, DC, September 1996.

Paperback 1 85490 351 9
128 pages, 141 illustrations
£21.95 DM57.00 $38.00
July 1996

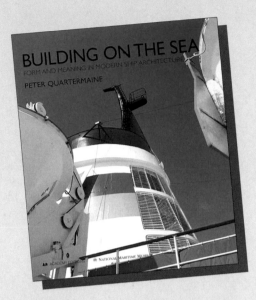

BUILDING ON THE SEA
FORM AND MEANING IN MODERN SHIP ARCHITECTURE

Peter Quartermaine

- A unique study revealing the similarities between architecture and ships
- Published in association with the National Maritime Museum, London

Ships have always been familiar and functional machines to the few, and remote objects of fantasy to the majority: most of us, after all, live on land. Consequently, both the practical and symbolic significance of man's largest mobile structures remains largely unexplored. *Buildings on the Sea* navigates these uncharted waters, and considers the way in which, in the post-modern post-colonial era, the architecture and function of ships reflects broader cultural patterns.

This book, through its exploration of these issues, examines the function and appearance of ships as one aspect of twentieth-century architecture. Written in clear non-technical language, *Building on the Sea* is beautifully illustrated with high-quality photographs, drawings and plans, which are integral to the book's argument.

Hardback 1 85490 446 9
128 pages, 200 illustrations, 100 in colour
£29.95 DM85.00 $50.00
September 1996

MOSHE SAFDIE
Edited by Wendy Kohn

This detailed appraisal of world-renowned Israeli architect Moshe Safdie is long awaited. Since the Habitat scheme built in 1967, he has developed from strength to strength and, resisting specialisation, designed an astonishing range of buildings. With offices in Jerusalem, Boston, Toronto and Montreal, his projects span the globe, from Munich to Senegal, Damascus to Los Angeles. To accommodate the variety of typologies and locations, the book has been arranged thematically – 'Early Work', 'Rebuilding Jerusalem', 'Housing', 'Public Buildings', 'Education and Research', 'Mixed-Use Facilities' and 'City Design' – with sketches, illustrations and photographs of some of his most recent projects, including the stunning Vancouver Central Library, Canada.

Contributions to the book include critical assessments by Peter Rowe, Michael Sorkin and Paul Goldberger.

With nearly 800 illustrations, mainly in colour, this is an exceptional volume which will complement any architect's personal library.

Hardback 1 85490 453 1
320 pages, nearly 800 illustrations, mainly in colour
£49.50 DM147.00 $85.00
July 1996

Further information can be obtained from Academy Group Ltd, 42 Leinster Gardens, London W2 3AN, Tel: 0171 402 2141, Sales: 0171 402 3442 Fax: 0171 723 9540, or from your local sales office.

National Book Network, 4720 Boston Way, Lanham, Maryland 20706, USA. Tel: (301) 459 3366 Fax: (301) 459 2118

VCH, Boschstrasse 12, Postfach 101161, 69451 Weinheim, Federal Republic of Germany, Tel: +49 6201 606 144 Fax: +49 6201 606 184

S,M,L,XL
Rem Koolhaas and Bruce Mau
010 Publishers

On silver, glossy paper, the back cover introduces the reader to the 1,346 pages in hand as follows:

This massive book is a novel about architecture. Conceived by Rem Koolhaas – author of *Delirious New York* – and Bruce Mau – designer of *Zone* – as a free-fall in the space of typographic imagination, the book's title, *Small, Medium, Large, Extra Large*, is also its framework: projects and essays are arranged according to scale. The book combines essays, manifestos, diaries, fairy tales, travelogues, a cycle of meditations on the contemporary city, with work produced by Koolhaas's Office for Metropolitan Architecture over the past twenty years.

This much is certainly true, but what are we to make of this *magnum opus*? Well, scale is at least an issue. Using a layered narrative we are taken through a variety of projects:

Small. An individual house. Villa Dall'Ava, Paris.
'they lived there happily ever after. One Saturday morning they counted 30 people outside, looking in . . .'
Medium. Netherlands Dance Theatre, The Hague. A chronology from commission to completion.
'Innocence, Panic, Simulation, Battlefield, Disbelief, Approach, Engagement, Suspense, Compression, Immersion, Performance, Release.'
Large. Sea Terminal, Zeebrugge.
'How to inject a new "sign" into a landscape that – through scale and atmosphere alone – renders any object both arbitrary and inevitable?'
Extra Large. Ville Nouvelle Melun-Sénart, France
'A heartbreaking obscenity to have to imagine a city in such a place.'

All of these, and much more, chronicle an extraordinary diverse and rich portfolio.

Images of work are often accompanied by a text: some project descriptions, others relating to the process of design; a 'dear diary' of Koolhaas's anxieties from 29th April to 2nd July 1989, as the office worked on the Très Grande Bibliothèque competition. In other cases the connection between image and text is less clear; a dialogue from Beckett's *Waiting for Godot* overlaying photographs of the Rotterdam Kunsthal II, each obscuring, or perhaps illuminating, the other.

Autonomous texts are embedded between the projects, although most of these will be familiar to the OMA enthusiast, having been previously published elsewhere. They include extracts from *Delirious New York*, *Globalisation*, *Bigness or the Problem of the Large*, *What Ever Happened to Urbanism?*, *Singapore Songlines*, etc. All are important pieces and their collection together reinforces this view.

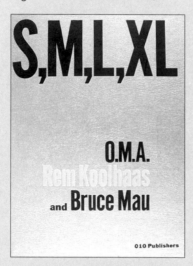

Accompanying the shifts in scale, an alphabetically ordered series of quotations appears sporadically from beginning to end. This is a kind of idiosyncratic architectural glossary, with the citations given at the end of the book so that the reader is unaware of the definition's author. Hence:

Blonde: But I say, just as in footwear, we need beautiful, in addition to mildly useful buildings. My pavilion I should wish to be compared to [a] high-style, high-heel evening slipper, preferably satin – a pleasure giving object, designed for beauty and the enhancement of human, preferably blonde, beauty.
(Philip Johnson, 'Full Scale False Scale', *Writings*, Oxford University Press, New York, 1979)
Colour: Rusty wants to be Coco. Sandy wants to be Cherry. It's so easy to be somebody else with Harmony Hair Colour – just one wash in and six washes out. It's as simple as that.
(Harmony Hair Colour, advertisement, *Cosmopolitan*, September 1991)

Interlaced within the structures are a series of, again notionally unconnected, images, including car debris in a Parisian street (*circa* 1968), a detail of Tiepolo's *Apollo and the Continents* and an advertisement for men's underwear.

Having disentangled the various threads running through the book you will detect the rather structural approach that this viewer has adopted in order to explain the contents, but this is to miss both the point and potential of the book. The introduction inform us that architecture is a chaotic adventure and that coherence is cosmetic, or the result of self-censorship. In *S,M,L,XL* contradictions are not avoided and we are told the book can be read in any way. In fact, both the enormity of the text and the structural juxtaposition offer readers the opportunity to navigate their own path, jumping between the structures, to create a personal reading. Similarly, Anthony Vidler made an analogy between this book and the hypertext links of a CD-ROM. This is all very well, but my concern is that such a strategy leads necessarily to 'sound bite' content, and invites the reader into a banal superficiality, analogous to aimlessly wandering the Internet or channel-hopping through television feeds. Any reader unfamiliar with OMA's work will find it difficult to engage in the fullness of their architecture; the content being obscured and sometimes trivialised as a result of the structure. For such individuals I would recommend more focused texts: *Delirious New York* is an important work in its own right, and was recently reissued; *El Croquis* 53 provides a good summary of built and unbuilt projects from 1987-92, and perhaps most importantly, *Architectural Design* profile 5, 1977, gives the most vivid insight into the ideas upon which much of the work is premised.

As for the current tome, I regret that it will only serve to further indulge those already seduced by OMA's work at a superficial level, and will no doubt give further fuel to those determined to dismiss it. The argument that this is an architecture of 'surface' is still further supported by the evident lack of scale at a detailed level; small-scale models miraculously emerge as buildings, and matters of materiality, structure, construction and environmental control are conspicuous through their absence. It is true that these issues have never been at the fore in the chronicling of OMA, but surely this project provided the opportunity to offer more. I cannot labour this point enough. We are told nothing of the exquisite minimal detailing of the House for Two Friends, Rotterdam; instead we are tossed an incomprehensible fragment of the various structural methods – in the form of an engineer's notebook calculations – considered for the Très Grande Bibliothèque.

My own reading reaffirms that I have always been engaged by the intelligent and sophisticated rhetoric of OMA, and in many cases admire the architectural virtuosity that brings together theory and practice in one brilliant moment. I do, however, have no interest in much of the triviality, and see the emphasis of the familiar morphological conceptual narrative at the expense of the tectonic representation as a missed opportunity.

I started this by saying that scale was certainly an issue in this book. Koolhaas may not have lost his sense of scale, but I am forced to wonder if he still has his sense of proportion.

M Pearce

> This massive book is a novel about architecture. Conceived by Rem Koolhaas – author of *Delirious New York* – and Bruce Mau – designer of Zone – as a free-fall in the space of the typographic imagination, the book's title, *Small, Medium, Large, Extra Large,* is also its framework: projects and essays are arranged according to scale. The book combines essays, manifestoes, diaries, fairy tales, travelogues, a cycle of meditations on the contemporary city, with work produced by Koolhaas's Office for Metropolitan Architecture over the past twenty years. This accumulation of words and images illuminates the condition of architecture today – its splendors and miseries – exploring and revealing the corrosive impact of politics, context, the economy, globalization – the world.

ARCHITECTURE ON THE HORIZON

CDS ASSOCIATES, MODERNISSIMO CINEMA, NAPLES, ITALY

Architectural Design

ARCHITECTURE ON THE HORIZON

TOM KOVAC, CAPITOL NIGHTCLUB, MELBOURNE, AUSTRALIA
OPPOSITE: MUF (PREVIOUSLY JULIET BIDGOOD LIZA FIOR ARCHITECTS), GYMNASIUM, WATERLOO, LONDON

ACADEMY EDITIONS • LONDON

Acknowledgements

All material is courtesy of the authors and architects unless otherwise stated. We are grateful to the architects for their enthusiasm and interest in the project. On behalf of Eichinger oder Knechtl we would like to thank Ingerid Helsing Almaas, author of *A Guide to Recent Architecture in Vienna*, Ellipsis Publishers (London), 1994, for her project texts and interview with the architects. We would also like to thank Gerlind Fichte for her help in the translation of several pieces of text, and our thanks also go to Dennis Sharp Architects, Guiseppe Dell Aquila, Charles Correa and Michael Rotondi for their assistance.

Photographic Credits: All material is courtesy of the authors and architects unless otherwise stated. Attempts have been made to locate the sources of all photographs to obtain full reproduction rights, but in the very few cases where this process has failed to find the copyright holder, our apologies are offered. Arthur Blonk GKf *pp64-65*; døgl-cherkoori *p17 (above left)*; Herman van Doorn GKf *pp66-67*; Georges Fessy *pp5, 22-23*; Luuk Geertsen *p69 (above left and right, centre and below left)*; Nigel Haynes *p81 (above)*; Jorg Hempel *pp32-35*; David Hewitt/Anne Garrison *pp94-95*; Andy Keaton *p74*; Andy Keate *pp84-87*; Jason Lowe *pp2, 81 (below), 82-83*; Trevor Mein *pp3, 8-11*; Jean Marie Monthiers *pp28-30*; André Morin *pp20-21*; Olivieri *pp46-47*; Josh Pullman *p73*; Bharath Ramamruthan *pp42 (below), 43 (below)*; Erwin Reichman *pp14-15*; Tomas Riehle *pp36-37*; Margherita Spilutini *pp12-13, 17 (right), 18-19*; Scott Smith *inside covers, pp88-91*; Antonio Trimarchi *pp1, 51*; Rajesh Vora *p4 (right)*; Derk Jan Wooldrik *pp3, 63*; Chiaki Yasukawa *pp57*; Kim Zwarts *p61 (above right)*

SIV

We would like to thank Mike Johnson of SIV and the RIBA Architecture Centre for sponsoring the exhibition 'Architecture on the Horizon', 14 August-21 September 1996, at the RIBA Architecture Centre, London.

Front Cover: Herault-Arnod Architectes, Nomad, a conceptual architectural project produced for the exhibition *Application and Implication* at the MAGASIN-CNAC, Grenoble, May 1993 (photo: André Morin)
Inside Covers: Daly, Genik, Salzman Residence, Tarzana, California

EDITOR: Maggie Toy
EDITORIAL TEAM: Iona Baird, Stephen Watt, Jane Richards
ART EDITOR: Andrea Bettella CHIEF DESIGNER: Mario Bettella DESIGNERS: Alex Young, Alistair Probert

CONSULTANTS: Catherine Cooke, Terry Farrell, Kenneth Frampton, Charles Jencks, Heinrich Klotz, Leon Krier, Robert Maxwell, Demetri Porphyrios, Kenneth Powell, Colin Rowe, Derek Walker

First published in Great Britain in 1996 by *Architectural Design* an imprint of
ACADEMY GROUP LTD, 42 LEINSTER GARDENS, LONDON W2 3AN
Member of the VCH Publishing Group

ISBN: 1 85490 257 1(UK)

Distributed to the trade in the United States of America by
NATIONAL BOOK NETWORK INC, 4720 BOSTON WAY, LANHAM, MARYLAND, 20706

Printed and bound in Italy

Contents

HERAULT-ARNOD ARCHITECTES, GYMNASIUM, MORESTEL, FRANCE

ARCHITECTURAL DESIGN PROFILE No 122

Architecture on the Horizon

INTRODUCTION
KESTER RATTENBURY

Whatever journalists may think, the format of architectural publications is not geared to the productions of young architects. Despite the media's guiding ideal of identifying the new, architectural books and magazines are generally set up to present the single building study – the monograph – and tend to show even its newest incumbents in the terms of the *faux*-retrospective. Along with the rest of the media, we are partial to our soap opera stories of the developments and vagaries of well-known characters ('What are Foster's doing now?'). It makes the writer's work of sifting an infinite world of activity for good material so much easier. Setting up new heroes in this galaxy is sophistically essential – and as dodgy as launching any new soap. What happens if they only do one fairly good building? What happens if they don't do any buildings at all?

The last is a particularly tricky point for the architectural media, because it takes a long time for complete, entire, new-build buildings (of the type generally accepted as 'real architecture') to attach themselves to young designers – a time lag which doesn't fit very conveniently into the journalistic-predictive drive. The pragmatic diversifications of young ambitious practitioners during recession arc commonly taken as insufficient evidence of the transition from the imaginary world of the student or the paper architect into the built architectural 'proof' of their ambitions. This situation is further complicated by the current argument of an increasing culture of visual sophistication in which architecture, film, advertising and electronic publishing are all operating in the same potent semiotic field of mixed-media practices, which include artists or writers, and behave accordingly. Editorial meetings on publications such as this are beset by the constant agonised question: 'But is it architecture?'

Often of course, it isn't – which is frequently, if not always, a good sign. Okay, architects claiming a new global diversity have been responsible for or involved with a lot of second-rate art and theory – as well as the occasional good bit – the whole of which has often been treated with great reverence by an overexcited and under-informed press. But this means that the architectural press will have to become better critics in related fields, and not that the work-related fields should be either ignored – or over-revered.

Moreover, the question of 'real' architecture is a peculiar one for a culture operating in some curious liminal state between absolute pragmatism and total fantasy, where unbuilt competition entries are defined as, and even mistaken for, buildings, while built interiors or installations do not count as architecture. Amongst the new polemic which surrounds some of this work – often coming from the same practitioners (like Muf or Fat), who are usually also teaching part-time – there is a new attention to this curious state of affairs: to the ambiguous nature of the architectural drawing; to the relationship of the architectural conventions of drawing, image, writing (the language in which architecture is usually discussed, described and commissioned) and the language of the cavity wall. On the relative drawing conventions of Decon and the damp-proof membrane. On the current evidence it is wrong to imagine post-digital architecture will disperse into the imagineers and the design-and-build. Of course, this theoretical attention to the medium itself may be its last decadent decline – but it doesn't look like it, either abstractly or practically.

The residual resistance of the architectural press to presenting things other than buildings is thus perfectly valid – both to see how far these residual or essential buildings are related to the digital, virtual, theoretical hyperbole which surrounds them and to examine these first putative buildings on their own ground. (electronic publishing will make this easier to cross-reference with other media sources, though a new confusion between the representation and the represented is inevitably on the cards.) However, the fairly strict architecture menu also allows examination of how such cultural arguments are borne out, how far such arguments have spread, and what effects this may appear to have on the buildings presented; and to look at this both within and between countries. (There seems to be, for instance, a new formal similarity between works in Vienna and London, whereas the last generation, whatever their architectural language, were definitely stylistically distinct.)

This issue of *Architectural Design* then operates within the normal ambiguous media fantasy. In the quest for the new but recognisable, it attempts to discover a new theme or movement – while showing work which does not necessarily conform to this. In the quest for the quality or sense of the building, it has to put forward a series of representations of a building. In search of international developments, it focuses mainly, but not entirely, on similar sorts of project in major cities in the developed world. As a prediction of the horizons of architecture, it more or less excludes most of the major changing issues: ecology; the development of the Eastern bloc; South Africa; the developing world; housing; politics; patterns of development, or funding, or commissioning. It predicates the organisation of information into a partly supported argument: for an architecture re-establishing its existential expressiveness within and through an increasingly sophisticated and diverse world. It focuses on the stylistic, formal and cultural obsessions of a small group of potentially influential practitioners working in a certain generation of fashionable work in the developed nations. It looks at some pictures of reasonably unfamiliar and pretty good buildings. Back to the soap opera. A new generation.

Driendl*Steixner, Platform, Office/Flat, Vienna

AUSTRALIA

TOM KOVAC

Tom Kovac is alone. His architectural dementia has no parallel in Australia. Only Brett Whitely with two lines could extract the essence of form that Kovac extracts from space. His curvaceous and taut sensual forms invert on themselves to create a continuity of lines like Kelly Slater or Martin Potter leave on a wave.

This Slovenian-born Australian architect's work is somewhat dispossessed amidst a litany of contemporary works whose addictions to Pop (Melbourne), bush junkieism (Sydney) or climate (Darwin) offer us only variations on a theme, sameness. But when Hundertwasser stated that 'the quickest way to hell is to draw a straight line', Kovac was listening. For here is something else.

Kovac's space of flows is not that of Gaudí, Steiner or Aalto, but of Brancusi or Noguchi. In contemporary architecture, Niemeyer is the closest referent, and only Gehry can dream of these forms . . . because this fresh and dynamic work denies the architecture of planes. It is seamless; spaces without shadow. Being and nothingness, empty and omnipresent.

With a career since 1990 in interiors and residential projects – Cherry Tree hotel (1990), Succhi shoe store (1991), both of which won RAIA Interior Awards, Gan House (1993), Island House and Atlas House (1996) – it is not surprising that Kovac's architecture is handled from the inside out.

Over five years, Kovac's work has simultaneously stripped and added a new dimension to architecture. The work does not derive from theory, rational argument, semantic icon, or nuts and berries: nor is it an urbanist's vision. It is, of and unto itself, emotionally charged work and one man's shot at injecting the programme into an obsession with pure form.

It is as simple and abstract as that.
Dale Jones-Evans

The progression from intangible concept to solid reality fascinates me. Architecture is difficult: permits, politics, clients, budgets, delays. All of my projects have antagonised the planning authorities here in Melbourne. I spend a lot of time formulating strategies to help get the work past conventional thinkers and outmoded regulations. Can architecture express culture? Can architects diagnose and prescribe? I believe architecture is critical and intuitive: the trick is to know where you're coming from.
Tom Kovac

The spatial plasticity of Kovac's work is a conscious response to his conception of the Australia condition, and a deliberate rejection of the 'cargo cult' approach to architecture which prevails amongst those who choose to work within the thin transmissions of Modernist precedent.

The work seeks to reveal the new in the new world, and sets itself in contradistinction to the imported legal frameworks which define Australian space. The forms that he uses may have their own Modernist architectural precedent in Kiesler's Endless House (1950), but unlike that free-standing work, much of Kovac's work presses against the orthogonal constraints that surveyors and planners have laced over the Australian city – constraints that mock the vast expanse of the island continent and reflect the crabbed social models that are the heritage of the colonial period.

Kovac's studio is filled with models of flowing idealised spaces, multiple utopias of worlds that could be – were we to give priority to our own experience rather than importing other people's histories.
Professor Leon van Schaik

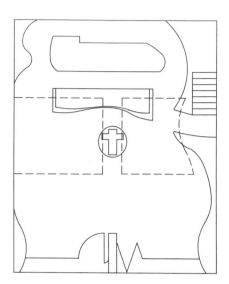

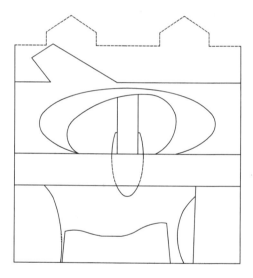

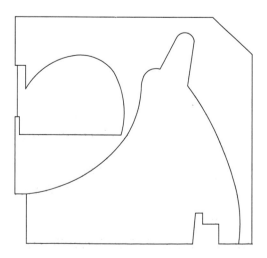

FROM ABOVE: Plan; cross-section; section

SAPORE

Melbourne, Australia

Located on a sweeping roadway overlooking Port Phillip Bay, the project fuses together the existing and the inserted interior through the creation of a seamless spatial mass.

The unusually low entry ceiling intensifies the interface between interior and exterior. A soaring ceiling unifies the two-level dining space. The expansive fluid volume is anchored by an existing beam, which forms a bridge connecting dining areas. Stair and other utilities are contained within the wrapped skin. The spare white ceiling opens to two deep elliptical spaces which provide natural light and a visual link between the two floors.

The central space is grounded by a black concrete bar which arrests its fluid surrounds.

GAN HOUSE

Melbourne, Australia

The programme is 100-square-metre addition to an existing Victorian house. The design assails many accepted assumptions concerning context, spatiality and habitation. It is conceived as an autonomous entity, tied to the existing structure by a glazed compression zone. Internal space is carved out of the mass of the external volume, blurring relationships between inside and out. The addition aims to generate its own dialogue with the urban fabric, asserting its presence and mysterious prehistory.

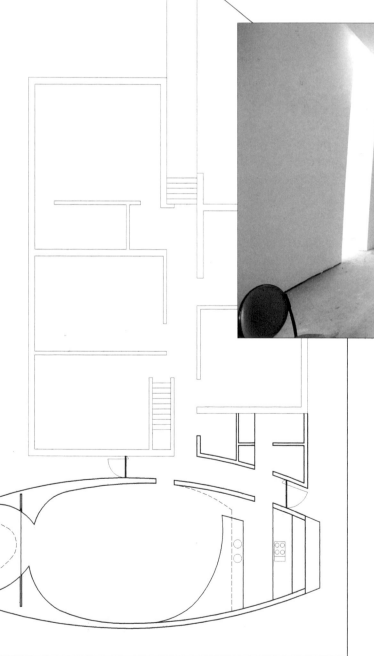

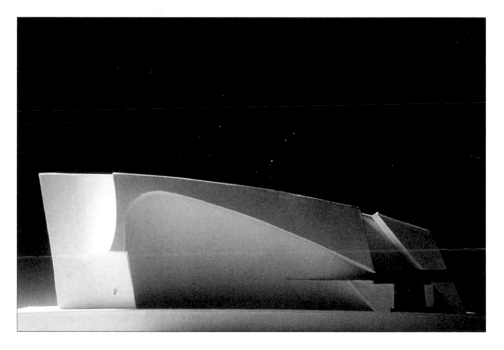

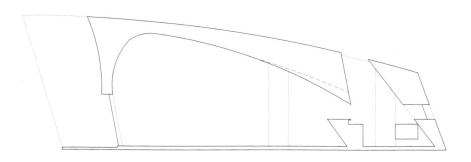

OPPOSITE: Plan; RIGHT, ABOVE AND CENTRE: Model sections; BELOW: Section, with living room to left and kitchen to right

AUSTRIA

DRIENDL*STEIXNER

Driendl*Steixner do not tell stories, they divide connections (also language) into elementary construction units before they restore them again.

The bar Skala has many corners and edges. None of the materials deceive about the fact that the night will be long and cool. At the entrance there is a light-sculpture: red spotlights generated at random slide across the floor and walls. There is no final stage and no encounter. The transparent 'standard solar house' is light-flooded, built of wood, stone, glass and steel. It adapts to its surroundings; stores energy in water and basalt. Both rooms formulate an unequivocal position. The parameters are technology, economy and ecology. It should be possible to adapt the house to a varying utilisation – such as the wall with racks, 'Magic Wall'. Besides its function as a solid place to store things, it takes on the many tasks of demarcation and structuring. Driendl*Steixner work on model solutions for analysed basic utilisation. They also produce films. They are directed according to defined criteria, a fixed number of sequences, the directive possibly sketched and . . . what a surprise! They are as light as a feather, suited for the cheerful science. No sentence is finished, no gesture completed. It contains an analysis of talking about architecture, the reduction and concentration of key positions which are manifested in word-fragments as well as posture and gesture. Film can apply a comparable de-composition/composition principle to ascertain an exemplary architectural attitude. By camera movement, simulated traverses, overlayings, sight angles, repetitions and metric installations, film analyses (not describes) architecture with pictures and tones. The films of Driendl* Steixner are educational films. The film on the preservation of monuments, Clip on

Denkmal, is a mathematical architectural time/space structure. 64 photographs (picture halves) can be exposed on one (35 millimetre) film. The square of 64 is the formal basic grid of the film. The tracks are put on top of each other according to this script. The educational statement on the preservation of monuments cannot be put in words, it takes place in 64 times 64 squares. Also Driendl*Steixner use videos to screen their films. They expose, produce and experiment with 35 millimetre films. The anachronistic and labour-intensive strategy is a comment on the belief in progress, in the unlimited possibilities of the 'new media'. Most of their picture material is collected with the camera; individual photographs in a sequence, unobtrusive, quick and self-controlled.

Driendl*Steixner are planning an instructive project in order to make the town visible for its inhabitants and users. Plans, sketches and real photographs of the metropolis (Vienna, Tokyo, New York, Belgrade) are structured in various scales and according to specific (self-developed) parameters, time dimensions analysed in space, and vice versa, space dimensions in time. A means of self-expression shall be developed, using slides, films and acoustic information, which facilitate a sensitive transparency of the phenomenon of urban planning, urban development. They are preparing a lecture on this theme. It will be a concentration of space/time acting offensively at the perceptual thresholds of the audience. The project is very concrete, something it shares in common with the artists' other projects. Although they often appear to be separate and marginal, they are never intended to be merely meta-phorical, linguistic games, but literally concrete. Only a few years ago a project by Driendl*Steixner annoyed a local

planning committee. The project was to build a house on top of a house, removing the roof of the first house so that it could be used as a basement for a second house with roof and side terraces. A concrete idea to concentrate high-quality housing in the centre of the town. A few years later the annoyance it caused to the local authority (which refused planning permission) is completely obsolete. The public/servant way of thinking had to give in. It might be that the urban project will be misunderstood as an art project (and classified as insignificant), and passed from one authority to the other until they realise that this is a necessary starting-point. How can decisions, space/time dimensions and the network of urban semantics be analysed, made sensually perceptible and noticeable? The success or failure of such projects will determine whether participatory models have a realistic future. They will set the conceptual level on which decisions can be considered and discussed. Last but not least, they will decide what should be built for whom and how.

OFFICE RENOVATION

Vienna, Austria

In renovating their office in Vienna, the architects have incorporated simple tectonics and structural materials into the design of the space. The practice have developed furniture and storage prototypes for use in specific and non-specific interior spaces for offices, banks and their own studio. These include moving walls ('Magic Wall'), doors and windows. There is as much attention to individual details in the construction of these elements as there is in the concept for the whole element or the individual spaces. This light-filled interior, with exposed concrete columns and burnished steel fittings, contains many unique elements, but also shows the development of a particular aesthetic.

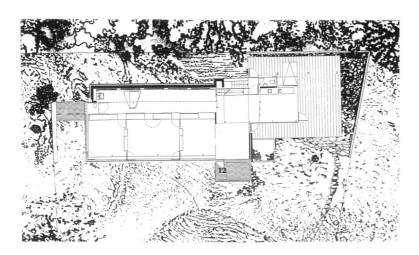

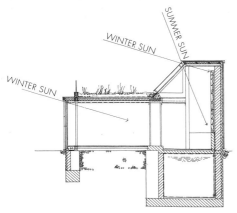

OPPOSITE, FROM L TO R: Ground floor plan; roof plan; daylighting section

STANDARD SOLAR HOUSE

Tulln, Austria

This house is the prototype for a production series solar house. Its modular planning concept allows a wide variation to suit local geography and topography, and can offer floor space from 130 to 200 square metres. Built-in cupboards maximise the available storage space. Aesthetic standards will not suffer through prefabrication.

The building uses the advantages of solid construction (thermal storage capacity) and light steel and wood (maximum volume with minimum materials). The insulated south facade admits light and warmth. External aluminium louvres protect against overheating from solar radiation in summer. Hollow-core sliding panels inside can be drawn across at night and in winter to give added thermal insulation. The opening parts of the transparent facade are cork-insulated wooden sandwich boards. The planted roof protects from the heat in summer and acts as insulation in winter. Energy from solar radiation is collected in active solar absorbers in the massive rear wall of the house, directed through a south-facing rooflight. The heat is transferred to a 70-square-metre water store. Active and passive solar elements lead to reduced consumption of fossil fuels.

EICHINGER ODER KNECHTL

Gregor Eichinger and Christian Knechtl in conversation with Ingerid Helsing Almaas
There is no salvation, no universal truth, no authority. Everything is possible. And the modern city, the purpose of which is to give you everything, simultaneously denies you the comfort of the right answer. The resulting contradictions are intolerable, and particularly painful in a city which still relies on its imperial past to give meaning to its physicality. So, in the context of the Austrian capital, the work of Gregor Eichinger and Christian Knechtl is a unique survival strategy. They grab hold of anything they can, *anything,* and mould it, knead it, look at it quizzically and then throw it away to grab hold of the next thing, like children, unimpeded by the pathetic heroism which frustrates so many ambitious architects. They take part in the city they live in, they give it (or try their damnedest to give it) their books, projects, places, buildings, parties, visions, thoughts.

Gregor Eichinger: Eichinger oder Knechtl are a special office in Vienna, because we were really the first to work in different directions – graphics, design, architecture and city planning. We did the cover for *Falter* [Vienna's weekly events guide] for a long time, which was interesting because it was like city planning research for us. It was fun. We are free to pick things from one place and apply them to another situation. If there is an obstacle in a certain direction we can go round and come from the back, from the other side. For us it is not so important to have an ideology in the way architects like to have: we have a manifesto but it's much more intangible, like water. Floating, you know? We are moving, doing several projects at the same time which are completely different, in different professional directions. But the thing is, we try to do it in an architectural way, not as architects are supposed to do them, but as we think architects could act. So we work on exhibitions, where we design the exhibition but we also do all of the scientific research, and we have graphics and book covers. There are also bars and living spaces, and a video project we started some time ago – this is normal for

us; it is a normal office schedule.
Ingerid Helsing Almaas: Are you fascinated by hi-tech?
Christian Knechtl: Of course, if you mean working with new technologies to do research, which is very important. The problem is that Austrian companies are not thinking in that direction. But they will have to.
GE: It will become a main area of interest and we have to bring it to a certain level, which is also an aesthetic thing. The ecological ideas that are coming into architecture must have an appeal, like the current consumer advertising for cars or shaving foam. I'm sure it's possible.
IHA: What does ecology mean? To some people ecology means nature conservation, but this is perhaps not the most interesting concept of ecology.
GE: No. We would rather turn it around, and say you don't have to care for nature, you have to care for mankind: if we carry on the way we're at doing the moment, we might accumulate all the wealth we need but we will kill ourselves.
IHA: What is the next project you are working on?
CK: There are lots of things. We are producing a newspaper. We have collected articles on architecture and science, and now we're giving them a new shape, to show the different perceptions. That will be a fun project. I see it as a recycling project too. As an ecological project.
IHA: Are you doing it for a commission?
CK: No, we are doing it for ourselves. We do it for architecture. (laughs)
GE: It's for the world. (laughs)

UNGER & KLEIN WINE SHOP
Vienna, Austria

A small wine shop in a quiet area towards the back of the inner city, in which the existing space is rendered and painted white, a background for a civilised theatre of drinking. The materials are very simple: varnished furniture board; welded and galvanised steel frames with standard profiles; and fair-faced concrete. The refinement is in the way the shop is run: the mixture of buying and drinking, eating from the display table and hiring the storeroom for parties. The room is self-consciously liberated from the normal habits of the city.

JEWISH MUSEUM REMODELLING

Vienna, Austria

The construction of a new Jewish Museum in the middle of Vienna, just off Graben, the main tourist shopping street, is an important addition to the culture of the city. Eichinger oder Knechtl's contribution, following an invited competition, is the reorganisation of the old Palais Eskeles to house a museum not only for Jewish religion and history but also for contemporary Viennese Jewish culture. The inner courtyard has been roofed over by a curved glass roof which covers the main room of the new museum: an empty space, housing only a small but valuable collection of religious arte-facts. The two upper floors are connected to this space by open galleries.

FRANCE

HERAULT-ARNOD ARCHITECTES

Since the European city is no longer growing at an accelerated pace, a new way of thinking about the role of architectural work is required today, concerning in particular the urban heritage of the last few decades. We have certainly experienced the world of the endless city, and it is now appropriate to think more in terms of the territory than of the city. We are confronted with a space that is no longer homogenous and organised, but is rather an often unconnected territory with different types of logic at stake: this world is designed piece by piece, and changes constantly under economic and social pressures. Any belief in unity is illusory. As we work today, we must be guided by the concept of heterogeneity.

Within this context, the architect no longer invents a microcosm reflecting a cosmos of divine essence, nor a new content in the image of a modern man. He builds on what exists already, with the goal of finding a new balance which will provide an element of humanity and mystery. Within this framework, our buildings are based on an intervention strategy that is characterised by a certain boldness of objects and a subtle, almost surgical, contextual integration.

This process functions equally well in urban, semi-urban, and natural environments. In all cases, the procedures are the same: embrace the pre-existing, do not force, but rather, reveal the strengths and specific nature of places. The project becomes a revealer of its surroundings, a key to interpreting the site. This involves a quasi-empirical design method, which places an emphasis on volumes and model tests, excluding any *a priori* image.

Our projects do not necessarily reveal at first sight the manner of their integration into the environment; instead this is gradually suggested by a whole series of physical and material relationships that become perceptible as one moves around and inside the buildings.

In this respect, we are attempting to create a balance between the domains of thought and sensation; in other words, between concept and experience. Despite the pervasiveness of the mass media and the dominance of the screen and speed, architecture is losing its weight, its physical presence and relative permanence. It seems that modern man, in prioritising mechanics and the development of means of communication, has chosen to live in a mode of perpetual acceleration; to counter this, we must lessen the 'always faster' frenzy by prioritising the slow evolution of the energies of nature. Architecture, because it is immediately experienced, offers a potential for emotion that we cannot afford to lose.

TOURIST INFORMATION CENTRE
Mizoën, France

Three small communities in a valley of the French Alps wanted to interrupt the stream of tourists who pass by each year. Their idea was to build an information centre at the intersection of the main road and valley, something capable of enticing motorists to stop.

Bordered on one side by an overhanging precipice and on the other by a vertiginous dam, the site is exceptional. The decision was then taken to set the building above the road planting it in equilibrium between the rock and the void, thus offering visitors the unique view of an impressive vista. The structure is made of Corten steel which matches the brown tint of the nearby rocks, rich in iron oxides.

RIGHT: Section; BELOW: Plan

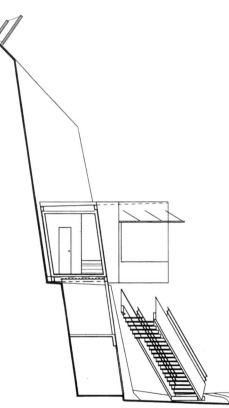

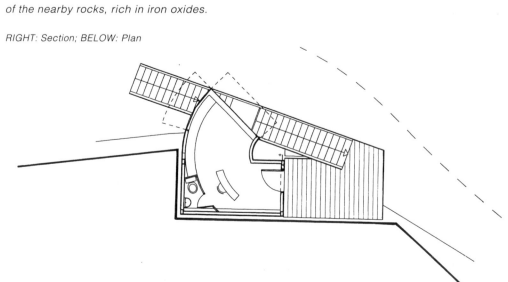

20

HIGH SCHOOL AND GYMNASIUM

Morestel, France

The building occupies a site on the edge of a village. 'A school in the countryside' was the theme. The project thus takes its logic from the presence of hedgerows tracing the lines separating the fields which, from aerial views, form a grid with a north-south axis.

The school and gymnasium themselves are sub-divided into volumes which are equally autonomous plastic entities. The interpretation of solids and voids gives the building an urban quality, taking its logic from the architectural panorama of natural stone, white concrete and copper, which goes brown then greenish as it oxidises. The building will gradually melt into the surrounding vegetation.

BELOW: Site plan; South-west elevation of high school; OPPOSITE BELOW: Sectional south-west elevation of high school

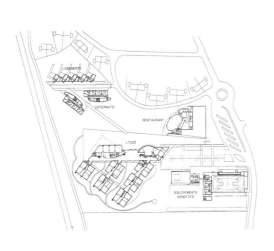

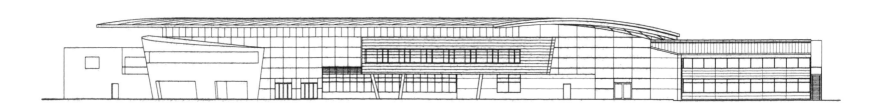

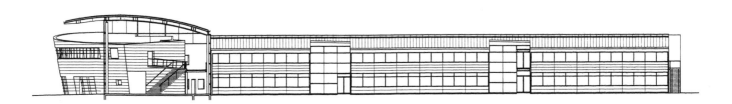

FRANCE

d ECO ï ATELIER

dECOi is a Paris-based architectural/ design atelier which was formed in 1991 in response to the Europan II housing competition. The rubric dECOi (the code used for the competition) has served as a leitmotif for various speculative architectural projects, often done in collaboration with people from other cultural disciplines. The generative nucleus of these disparate groupings is the partnership of Mark Goulthorpe and Zainie Zainul, whose differing cultural and disciplinary outlooks (one English, the other Malaysian) provide a curious dynamism, and a continuing evolution of ideas.

In large part these ideas have been pursued through a series of competition entries, both theoretical and professional, which has resulted in several accolades but little concrete work (winning entries include: Another Glass House Competition USA, Europan II Greece, La Casa piu' Bella del Mondo Italy, Nara/Toto World Architecture Triennale Japan). dECOi seem to view this simply as a necessary part of the formation of a practice in an architectural climate increasingly dominated (at least in France) by competitions: a sort of transition-point between education and professionalism. The competitions have provided a platform which identifies the group both from within and from without, which is just beginning to give way to the first commis-sioned work, be it architectural (three housing projects, at differing scale, in Asia) or conceptual (various installations or sculptural projects in Europe). In addition it has led to an invitation to run a design unit at the Architectural Association in London, which has enabled them to broaden greatly the scope of their research work, and has given rise to a series of conceptual projects (photographic, textual, technological, etc).

In a short a space of time the group has gathered an impressive list of prizes (including the Young Architects Forum in New York and Les Albums de la Jeune Architecture in France). This attests to the seriousness which underpins their dynamic and free-ranging activity, in both a cultural and geographic sense. They seem equally at home talking about ballet as the growth of fast cities in Asia, each of which may be used as a point of departure for an architectural reverie. Their work is light but diligent, and suggestive of a world of open boundaries – between countries as between disciplines. This is underscored by their invitation to represent France in the Venice Biennale in September 1996, which they hope will further assist their efforts to consolidate a professional presence in France.

The three projects presented here offer a glimpse of the spectrum of dECOi's production, from the abstraction of their conceptual work (Ether/i) to the more rigorous and exacting competition entries (Prosthesite), to the almost prosaic simplicity of their first 'real' projects (Ulu Langat Retreat). It would also seem to reveal clearly the link between theory and practice . . .

ETHER / i

This installation, for the United Nations 50th Anniversary 'Global Village' Exhibition in Geneva 1995, was produced as an international collaboration across many disciplines: Michael Saup (interactive artist); Joni and Jacopo (dancers of the Frankfurt Ballet); dECOi; Yayasan Seni; Kumpulan Guthrie (sponsors); Lawrence Stern (computer imaging); David Glover and Sarah Mildrem (Ove Arup Engineers); Optikinetics (metalwork).

The exhibition was intended to celebrate international co-operation, a theme which dECOi pursued both conceptually and practically – the object being produced in the interstices of disciplinary and geographic borders. It began with the coming together of a couple in a dance – tracing, with computer imaging, a duet of the radical Frankfurt Ballet. The object results not from the 'positive' trace of the dance, but from the difference between repetitions of the same sequence – a trace or fissure of failure which invokes a recessive or disappearing sense that carries into a material dissolution. The piece they characterise as a 'representation of loss', not negatively, but as expression of the inevitable reconfiguration of sense brought about by technological change.

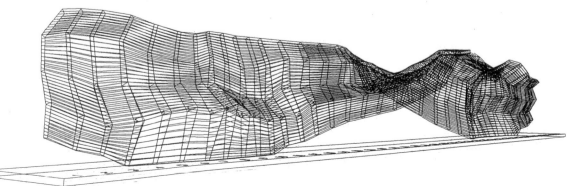

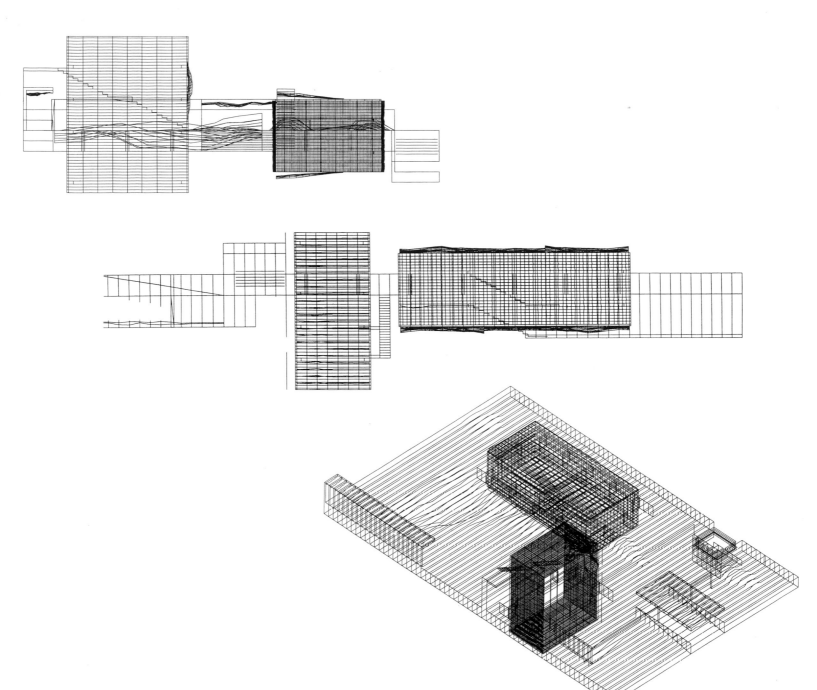

PROSTHESITE

Grand Prize in the Nara/Toto World Architecture Triennale 1995

The competition called for speculation on the theme of genius loci, *to which dECOi responded with a purely abstract and virtual site – a programmatic platform of sorts – an urban matrix which can be inserted anywhere (or any way – vertically, horizontally), and into which abstract architectural elements are plugged. The surfaces, whether at an elemental or urban level, are mute and continuous, yet small pulses of energy seem continually to be flickering across them, a sort of dynamic single-state surface, continually reconfiguring or recalibrating itself in response to contextual stimuli: an evidently interactive architecture.*

OPPOSITE BELOW: Perspective view; ABOVE: Elevation; longitudinal elevation; axonometric; plan view at 60 degrees

25

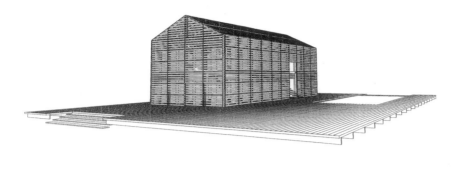

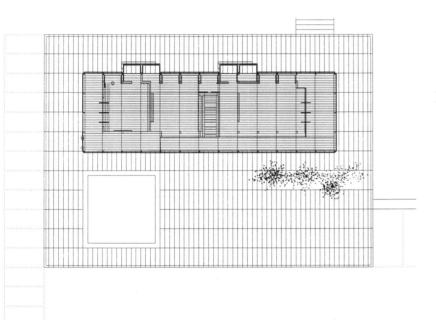

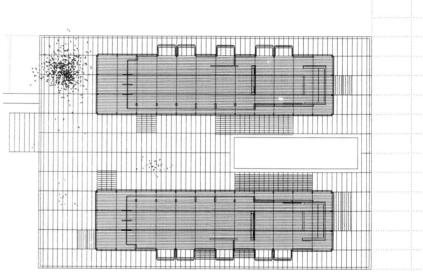

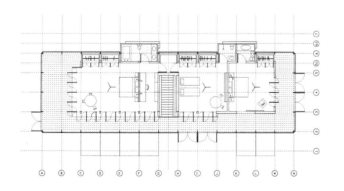

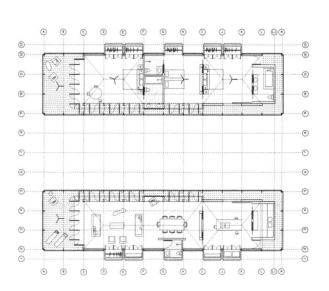

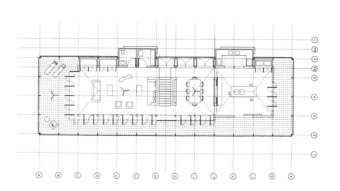

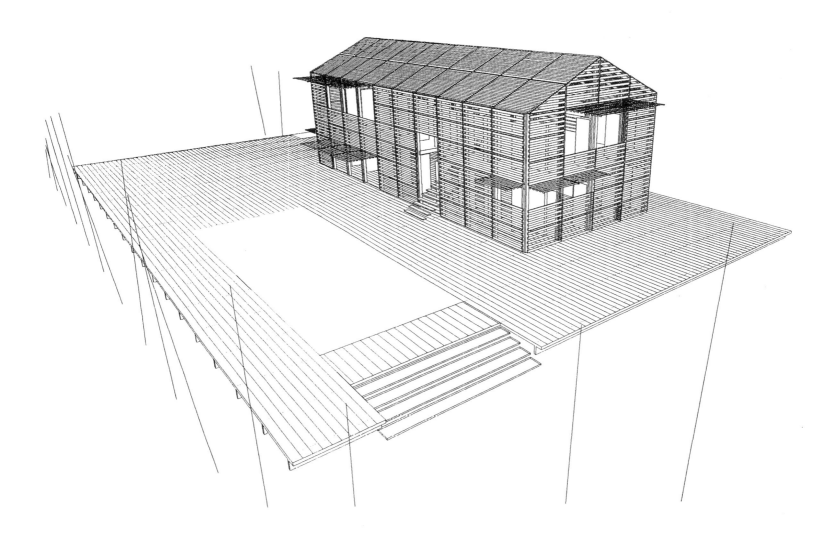

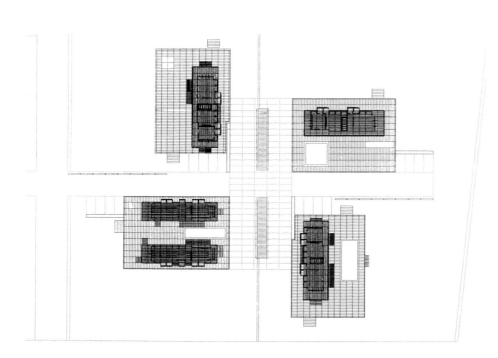

ULU LANGAT RETREAT

Near Kuala Lumpur, Malaysia

This project, one of dECOi's first direct commissions, is to provide 19 weekend retreat houses in an old rubber plantation just outside the capital, Kuala Lumpur. The design intends to offer a completely alternate lifestyle to that in the city, and is conceived as a series of stripped and elemental sheds, simple yet elegant, which are shrouded behind a veil of operable timber louvres. The rubber plantation is retained for its quality of filtered light, each house being placed on a plinth of wild grass with a black swimming pool. The interiors are spacious and open, naturally ventilated, and simply finished with painted concrete and timber in an attempt to maximise the spatial potential within the severely limited budget. Computer images by Thomas Modeen.

OPPOSITE, FROM ABOVE, L TO R: Perspective views of two-storey unit; two-storey unit plan; one-storey unit plans; two-storey unit, bedroom level plan and living plan; one-storey unit plans; ABOVE: Perspective view of two-storey unit; cluster plan

FRANCE

ATELIER SERAJI
(atelier + architecture)

Captain's Log: 2 June 1988
Location: Between London and Paris
Occasion: Opening of the exhibition 'INVENTER 89' at La Villette
Graduating from the AA in 1983 I work in London for five years. For two of these I try to set up my own practice in London: impossible.

I enter an 'ideas' competition in France and suddenly I find myself in Paris for the opening of the exhibition at La Villette. As I come out of the Grande Halle at 8.30 pm, the orange-red sky of Paris, the first follies of Bernard Tschumi shining on the green plate of the park, my lover and my success at the age of 30, all tempt me to stay in Paris.

I meet Adrian Fainsilbert at Roquelaure Reed Architects where I am working; he treats me in the French *maître-élève* fashion. I decide that I have to establish my own practice. I win a competition for R+R: they decide to share it with an old friend/associate. I leave the office and start teaching with Kirkor Kalayciyan, an associate of José Oubrerie (who worked for Le Corbusier in the 50s). Paris is sunny again. We talk about architecture and not *ego*.

In 1990 I win the competition for the renovation of a small flat in Paris and I register as a French architect: Atelier Seraji is born. Work is very scarce and I have to pay the expenses.

I continue teaching. Don Bates, an architect and a great friend, calls me up on Christmas Eve to give me a present. He recommends me for a short-list for another 'ideas' competition, for the American Center (temporary building) in Paris. The entry is a winner and the reality of Atelier Seraji begins on 1 April 1991.

Jean Paul Djalili works with me after I win the competition and gives me enormous support to realise my dream: a building that the French think impossible because it's not white – a building clad in chipboard in the middle of Paris! The American Center gives me exposure, publicity and, hence, legitimises me as an architect.

As Truffaut said, the first film is easy, it's the second that is the proof of creativity and singularity.

I am asked to teach at the AA and I accept. I feel that teaching is not only a duty but also that I have to offer to students my experience – I strongly believe that the space of theory is the practice of architecture.

Since the birth of the American Center, Atelier Seraji has gone through many rainy and sunny days – we have won competitions without building and we have lost competitions, although our scheme was better than the winning entry. Many young architects go through the same process.

The Atelier changes course in September 1994 when a former student of mine, Andres Atela, joins.

An associate since January 1996; he believes, as I do, that there are two main goals:

EXPERIMENTATION – the atelier is the space for experimentation.
ARCHITECTURE – the construction of the space of experimentation.
We both believe in the abolition of traditional hierarchies. Our plans, sections, and drawings attempt to express this. Our architecture deals with the 'other Modern' and the space of autonomy – an autonomy that allows the collective to exist without forcing it into a dogma.

The singularity of the work depends on the spatiality (*spatialité*) of the autonomous structures: the same as Corb's cluttered table in an ordinary bistro and Hannah Arendt's pristine horizontal surface, the image of *res publica*.

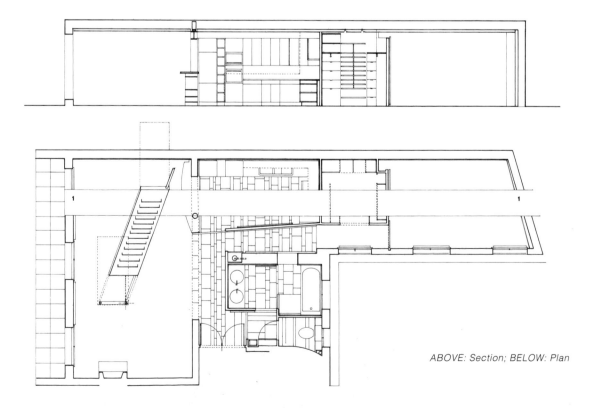

ABOVE: Section; BELOW: Plan

PRIVATE APARTMENT

Paris, France

This commission was for a small 100-square-metre flat in the 5th arrondissement of Paris, located on the fifth and sixth floor of a typical turn-of-the-century Parisian block. The lightness of the structure and the original I-shaped plan of the flat – lit from both the street court-yard facades – gave the opportunity for total freedom in the organisation of the plan.

The flat was originally divided into four small rooms on the lower level and one room on top. The renovation allows for three large rooms (living/dining, kitchen and bedroom) on the lower level, connecting to the work space on the upper level via a pivoting ladder-partition.

The kitchen opens to the dining area and is accessed through glass sliding doors from the entry hall.

AMERICAN CENTER
(TEMPORARY BUILDING)

Paris, France

The competition invited seven architects to submit ideas for a temporary building on a site in Paris opposite Frank Gehry's permanent building.

On a site of 540 square metres there were 21 trees. The building had to envelop the trees; the trees were the actors, the building its stage. It stands as a complex trace of many incidents and many confrontations.

The American Center building desired to be architecture: it demanded a dialogue; it allowed the inside to be outside; it presented a facade as two-dimensional. It allowed itself to be looked at, to be laughed at: it is present.

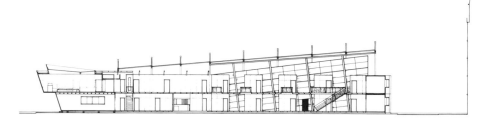

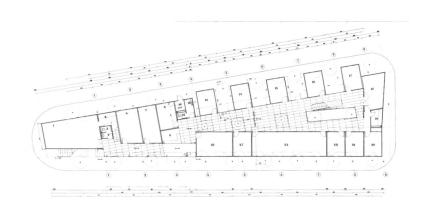

FROM ABOVE: Longitudinal section; ground level plan

MUSICON BREMEN

Bremen, Germany

How does one reconcile the collective celebration of the musical event with the individualistic act of listening? The coming together of people at a musical event should be an opportunity to give listeners a variety of sensations and experiences, capable of mirroring and encountering diverse individual expectations.

Music requires amplitude, musicians claim focus. A paradox in its entity. An experimental instrument for both public and professional use.

The large 2,500-seat Musicon could have been too deep or too vertical because of the narrowness of the site and the ambitious dimension of the programme. The asymmetrical shape of the expanded distorted amphitheatre accentuates the varying distances between the emission of sound and its reception by listeners. Particular musical characteristics are highlighted in the amphitheatre and multi-purpose balconies.

The geometry of the project underlines its hybrid characteristics: the vanishing points of the site and the individual entity of the musical events. The geometric configurations are balanced by the uniqueness of the volumetric core of the concert hall.

An order is distinguished by placing urban activities at the bottom and musical events at the top; progression from ground (stores, megastore and box office) to sky (the platforms of the media library, the balconies and the conductor's suite).

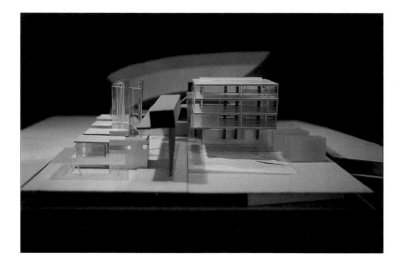

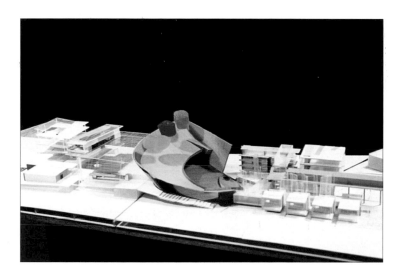

FROM ABOVE: Model views; section; site plan

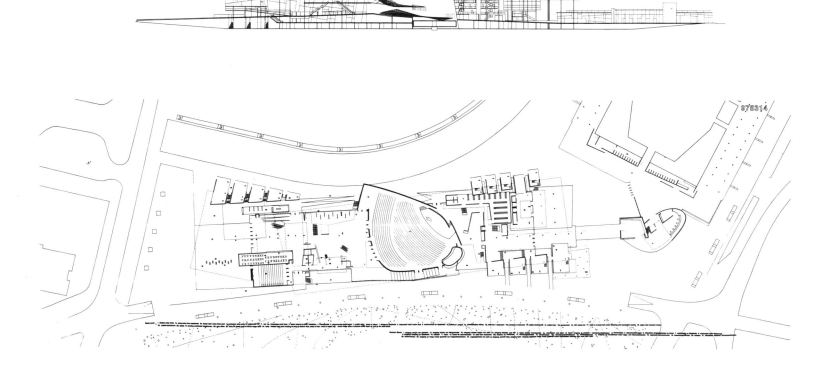

31

GRÜNTUCH/ERNST

Soft and Light

The work of Grüntuch/Ernst is optimistic. The projects delight in a search for the unknown and the discovery of new architectural possibilities: aesthetic, functional, technological and structural. The architecture is born of 'hi-tech' but then departs from it, offering significant development of this tradition.

Almut Ernst studied in Stuttgart under, amongst others, Peter Seidlein; Armand Grüntuch worked in London at Norman Foster's. Together they worked on a competition with Future Systems. Yet more experience was gained in Will Alsop's office and in studies at the Architectural Association in London and architectural schools in Aachen and Venice.

This grounding in hi-tech imparted a preference not only for materials such as glass, steel, cast iron and aluminium, but also for perfection of detail, freed from the formal dogma of machine aesthetics. Although the structure still informs the organisation, it no longer follows the rigid formal geometry of the grid. Space is defined mostly by the informal arrangement of three-dimensional structures.

Soft Order

In the design process, the structure is not treated as a stiff, rigid element, but as a softer, more malleable order or typological configuration, responding to environmental forces. These forces include climate, air currents, temperature flows and light-rays.

The forms remain open, non-deterministic. They are not shaped by any single factor considered in isolation, be it the manufacturing process, frame, function, climate or urban planning. Instead, the looseness of the forms allows the synthesis of these various forces.

During the design process the projects undergo a transformation in response to the specific local and environmental forces. The result is not an idealised volume, but a phenotype; as with living organisms, there is no perfect type (the embodiment of an ideal state), but rather a manifestation specific to the locality – the result of the building's own inner dynamics and outer influences.

The design is done mainly on the computer, which simplifies the dimensioning, visualisation and realisation of the double-curved forms of these freely shaped buildings. The introduction of the computer into the design process has also led to the development of a new aesthetic which, together with its associated architectural language, is representative of our society's present transition from machine age to information age.

It is not material value but rather information that is of importance today: the buildings become containers in which information is absorbed, produced, transformed and processed. As static objects, buildings are not in themselves information carriers, but pieces of hardware. As with computers, their performance and efficiency are the criteria by which they are judged.

Thematising the Skin

The thematising of the building envelope is not merely a question of aesthetics. Within certain architectural concepts, the skin can gain new spatial, structural and climatic functions. The facade as membrane becomes a climate modulator which regulates the flow of energy between internal and external environments. In almost every project by Grüntuch/Ernst the facade is conceived as a dynamic membrane. In the school for children with learning disabilities, the south-facing courtyard facade – made of metal panels, textiles and planting – not only tempers the climate but modulates the quality of light, shade and colour in the interior. Another interesting aspect of this project is the spatial function fulfilled by the facade, which acts not as a two-dimensional separation between inside and outside, but as a usable intermediate zone. The terraces between the inner and outer facade membranes create a protected external space connecting inside and outside. The adjustable louvres change in a dynamic way with the passage of the sun. The facades change according to the weather and the individual preferences of the users. They become indicators (like large barometers) of the different internal and external forces.

This is an architecture which overcomes some of the dogmas of classical Modernism, departing from the idea of the unity of form and function, functional determinism, and the pathological yearning for rationality, repetition, uniformity and the right angle.

In other respects this architecture captures exactly the spirit of Modernism; its joy in the unknown, its search for new techniques, new artistic and cultural possibilities, its optimism and enthusiasm for new technologies as well as its commitment to efficiency and comfort. It pursues a tendency towards reduction and abstraction, without denying the sublime hedonistic enjoyment of form.
Extract from a text by Phillip Oswalt
Translated by Richard Owers

HOTEL CONSUL CANOPY AND LOBBY
Berlin, Germany

The entrance to this small hotel in Knesebeckstraße can be seen from a distance spanning the pavement. The 60s flat roof, of corrugated plastic and wooden planks, was replaced by a canopy that Christopher McCarthy of Battle McCarthy describes as 'extremely simple, yet not elementary'.

The materials of the new canopy are sandblasted stainless steel for the structure, and glass for the canopy. Glass sheets with a span of 1,3 by 1.3 metres rest on the skeletal steel construction which consists of two main trusses 11.4 metres long and eight secondary trusses. Brushed steel is used for the column footings and for the cantilevered arms which support the glass. A steel U-beam connects the structure to the existing building. The welded roof elements were prefabricated in Austria and lifted by crane on to the composite columns.

As part of the streetscape seamlessly connected to the pavement, the new entrance canopy extends the public realm into the hotel foyer. The new interior, stripped of heavy curtains, dark furniture and columns, brings the period staircase and marble slabs back to life. The furniture is reduced to a minimum in order to keep the tight space light and airy.

In order not to obstruct the view of the stair, the obligatory key rack, situated behind the reception desk, is a simple glass screen.

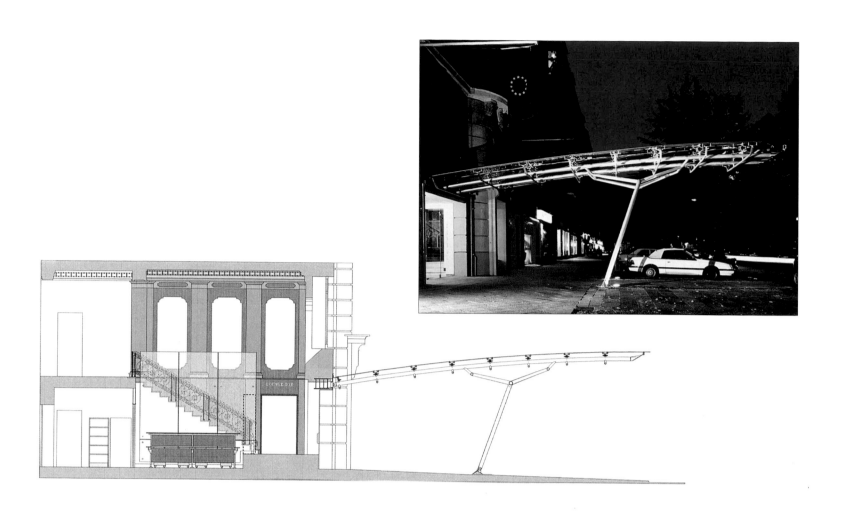

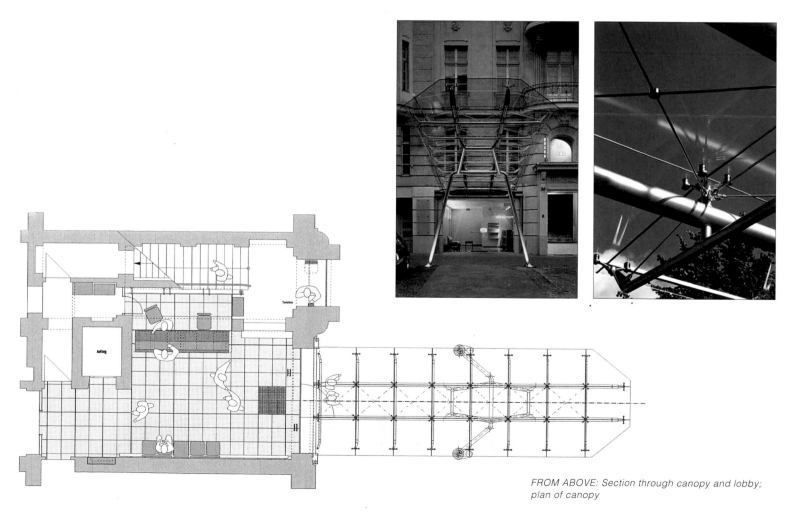

FROM ABOVE: Section through canopy and lobby; plan of canopy

GERMANY

PETZINKA, PINK UND PARTNER

The integration of the creative aspects of building technology and the concern for ecological and economic construction provide our architecture with a well-founded contemporary starting point.

This is far from an approach limited by the surface aesthetic, using only products developed to perform specific functions. It is not the ornament of a traditionally crafted form, but function synonymous with a future-oriented, mechanical and industrial evolution, expressed within an integrated building form.

Individual buildings in this category develop only with a growing perception. Each step of planning gives rise to aesthetic and functional ideas, which need to be worked out in order to direct, develop and, if necessary, correct the design and the approach to it. This kind of planning corresponds with the development of high-performance technical products.

Only by combining research, information, usage, knowledge and experience of a precise aesthetic vision is it possible to encompass the multi-faceted thinking of the present and obtain complex, durable solutions, in which each method and material is carefully chosen.

Our projects do not develop only from the abstraction of a 'good idea', but are products of an encroaching cooperation of all disciplines, each of which embraces many common technical interests.

The responsibility of the architect extends to the other participants in the planning process. The cooperation of manufacturers and professional engineers determines the success of the planning.

The result of the long-term planning and development of work is the generation of not only buildings of urban significance, but also visions for the 21st century.

STUDENT HOUSING

Wuppertal, Germany

To plan housing for students is to recognise the concept of social housing/living, integrating complex economic, constructive and social factors, without institutionalising the accommodation. The aim of the project is to 'produce' friendly family-type houses within a given budget, allowing young people to live together without giving up their privacy. Social interaction between the students is encouraged by the relationships of views and paths.

There are five houses which face each other, symbolising communication and tolerance. In addition, the surroundings are manipulated to 'soften' the boundary between the built form and nature.

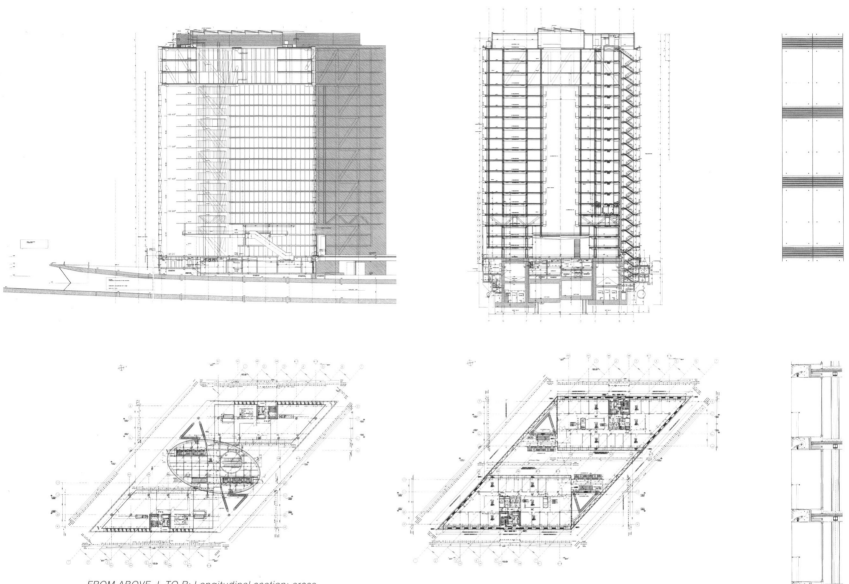

FROM ABOVE, L TO R: Longitudinal section; cross section; corridor facade; split-level plans; under construction; model; OPPOSITE, ABOVE: model; model detail at street level

DÜSSELDORFER STADTTOR

Düsseldorf, Germany

This project is situated over the entrance to a new underground tunnel which will help to alleviate the current traffic problems which separate the city of Düsseldorf from the Rhine. By lowering the Rheinufer street and taking the traffic underground, a new park will connect the old city centre with the river. A new 'creative' mile is proposed for the old harbour with offices, studios, media and advertising developments.

The Stadttor project is an office building which is designed to give a good quality of light, individual spaces and an attractive working environment. There will also be leisure facilities for employees to use in their free time.

The tower occupies a rhomboidal site and is split into two parallel towers with an atrium space between, which affords maximum views of the city.

INDIA

RAHUL MEHROTRA ASSOCIATES

Central to the approach of Rahul Mehrotra Associates is the importance of working simultaneously at many scales across related disciplines. The city of Bombay has served as a laboratory from which we have extracted lessons through our involvement with urban planning, conservation and research-oriented projects in the city. These experiences have in turn been consistently woven into our design approach. In fact, our work with urban issues in Bombay has informed our architectural design sensibilities and enabled us to evolve an architectural vocabulary that connects spatial and architectural elements from the past with a contemporary approach to building.

The practice strongly believes in the continuing relevance of the Modernist ethos which has had a great impact on contemporary India, both in terms of its rigour and in its ability to cut across the cultural differences that characterise India. For us the relevance of this ethos lies in its resilience as well as its capacity to adjust, adapt and absorb the architectural milieu of the locale.

However, the practice is conscious of the fact that, in India, Modernism also perpetuated the *tabula rasa* mind-set in the preceding generation – a mind-set that is raring to go in a kind of open context: 'I have seen the future and it works!' In response to this situation, the practice is committed to addressing not only of the contemporary urban landscape but also of our historic cities, identifying aspects that have continuing relevance for our emerging urbanism. In the coming decades a large majority of Indians will inevitably have to embrace urban living.

Beyond urban design and conservation, the work of the practice ranges from restoration and recycling projects to the design of interior spaces – from a staircase intervention to space planning for offices. The architectural projects similarly range from factories to single-family houses. Presently under construction are two office buildings, a sports club, an orphanage and a Rural Development Institute.

The practice, which comprises three associate architects, two architectural assistants and three administrative staff, recognises the significance of team work as integral to the production of architecture. All projects are therefore seen as collaborative efforts working closely with local associates in the cities where projects are located as well as with specialist consultants in Bombay.

BOUTIQUE AND STUDIO

Colaba, Bombay, India

The boutique is located in a historic building in Colaba where much subdivision had mutilated the facade into individual pieces. As work started on the area designated for the boutique, amazingly beautiful patinas of existing textures and colours were revealed below the vinyl flooring and laminated surfaces.

When the false ceiling was removed, and the paint was burnt off the original ceiling was revealed as teakwood; the vinyl floor was stripped away to expose red and ochre Minton tile flooring. In the course of the work, parts of the facade were discovered to be still in place. It was decided to restore the facade and to add elements such as a rolling shutter and canopy in copper. With oxidisation, the copper will develop its own patinas, to complement those of the existing space.

A studio was inserted in the form of a mezzanine with a connecting stair. The shell of the boutique was restored with compatible new elements carefully inserted without conflicting with the original architecture of the space.

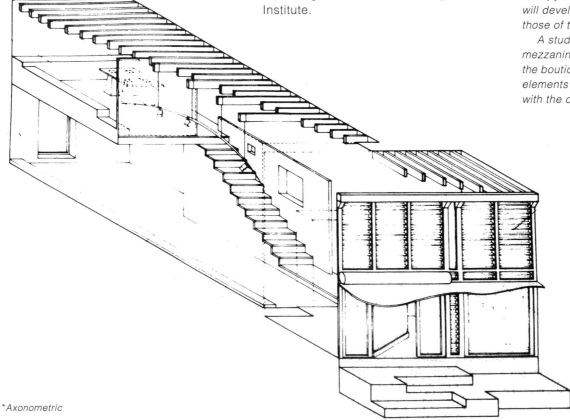

*Axonometric

HOUSE ON A FARM

Near Baroda, India

The issue was how to design a large house for clients who are essentially very urban people in a rural context – on a farm. What might be the appropriate aesthetic?

The entire house is positioned to occupy the whole shorter edge of the rectangular site, to create a buffer between the farm and the neighbouring plots off the other road. Strategically this also maximised the open space in front of the house.

Along the entry road is a very 'urban' facade; a more or less blank wall with a few small, seemingly random openings which were all the result of strictly functional requirements. On the farm side, a barn-like timber roof with traditional terracotta tiles creates a large veranda with various functions housed beneath it. The veranda space is a direct vernacular solution.

The interiors are sparse, with minimal furnishings, and the spaces are defined by movable partitions and bamboo chicks (bamboo blinds or screens which roll up manually).

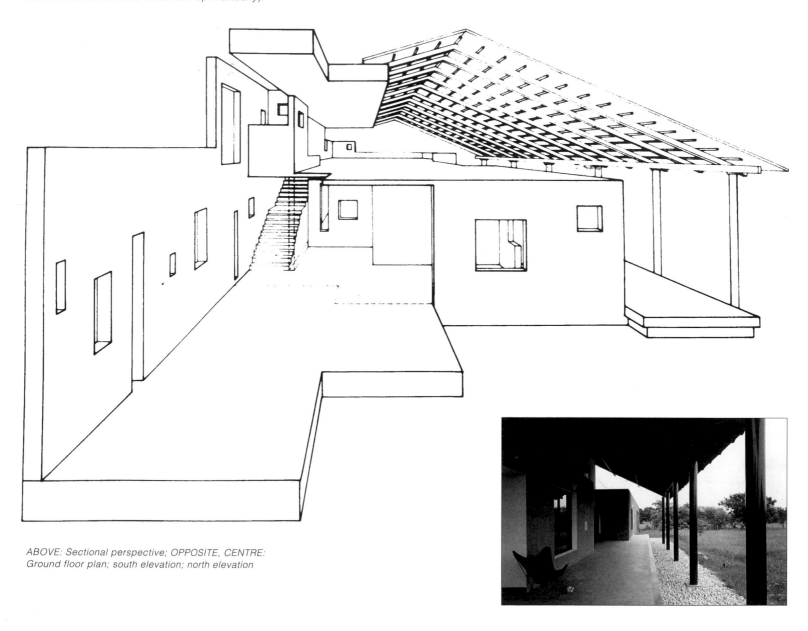

ABOVE: Sectional perspective; OPPOSITE, CENTRE: Ground floor plan; south elevation; north elevation

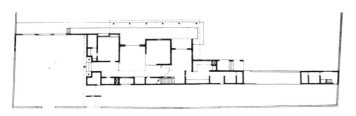

ITALY

ALDO AYMONINO

A shining darkness

Hanging on the wall of my living room there is a drawing representing an architectonic detail of a large outdoor enclosure surrounding a group of high trees. The drawing was done by Ludovico Quaroni, who was my professor in the final years of my university studies and the supervisor of my graduation thesis; the subject was the competition for a park in Bologna, which I had worked on with him and which won first prize. The date was 1984.

If that image has been given a place of honour in my home, it is not to preserve the sentimental memories of my student life, nor to celebrate professional success. To me that drawing has always represented the perfect synthesis of the two sides, one shining and one dark, of the job I have chosen to do.

On the one hand, I see the fact that the drawing was given to me as a present after the competition as a gesture of acknowledgement and appreciation of the work I had done. It stands for the meeting and unexpected friendship of the aged master and one of his young students; the proof that it is possible to work in an enthusiastic way; the validation of the hope that it is always possible to continue learning from someone.

On the other hand, it constantly reminds me, of repeated disappointment: the competition led to nothing – it was blocked by the Environmental Agency and today the renewal of the area is being done by an architect who did not even get into the second round of the competition. It recalls broken dreams; the subdued but ever-present pain of living and working in a country which chooses to be built by *geometri* – building technicians with secondary school diplomas who are permitted to design buildings up to three storeys – and engineering companies (about 75 per cent of the buildings built in Italy during the past 30 years have not been designed by architects, resulting in one of the lowest standards of architecture in Europe). It brings to mind the obtuse constraints set by people who are not interested in the quality of the project; and the mistrust and constant lack of acknowledgement of the work of younger architects. (I would

not be surprised if I were the oldest architect of the group invited to contribute to this issue of *AD*.)

At the age of 43, I remain, in comparison with my European colleagues, a professional youth; I have built hardly anything and my studio looks more like a workshop than the place where a mature professional carries out his job. Yet, when I show my work, it attracts attention.

Simultaneously, as a university tutor, I realise that, despite the objectively difficult academic situation, the work of the better students has no less intelligence or passion than that of their counterparts around the world.

In a country where the many (perhaps, too many) architects are under-used, employed in bureaucratic, unrewarding jobs, or living precariously close to the edge, an obsessive passion for one's job becomes a defensive weapon – against the ethical and professional bodies which are often marked by a lack of curiosity about the outside world and by the fear of losing their few acquired privileges. It is a weapon which allows one to maintain the ability to look around, to experiment with new ways to research and develop ideas, without accepting the end results, but instead going 'deep into the unknown to find the new' (Baudelaire). It allows one to go on dreaming in spite of it all and not surrender to cynicism; to try to stay young forever.

ASCENDING THE CITY

San Marino Republic, Schindler Prize 1994
With Maria Cicchitti, Giovanni Vaccarini, Francesco Ricci (structural engineer).

'No prisoners' – The main problem of San Marino undoubtedly relates to the means of access for the huge numbers of tourists visiting the old town centre.

The complex topographical structure of the area surrounding San Marino rules out the possibility of solving the problem with one single proposal. Therefore two proposals have been submitted to solve these problems: both complementary or alternative depending upon the political decisions and policies of the government of the Republic, they address the same global strategy, while dealing individually with specific locations. Generally, the choices could include the removal of private

traffic from the city centre by introducing a fast, efficient transport system; the redirection of traffic flow to areas that are not yet saturated with tourist facilities and services; to increase flow rates and introduce simpler transport systems (trams, shuttle buses, multi-storey parking); to relieve the city centre of the siege of tourist buses and private vehicles.

The two proposals offer different solutions in terms of transport options and means of access. The solution for the competition area (scheme 1) was to integrate a long mechanised route between the Baldasserona car park and the Piazza Borghesi, overlooking the Cava dei Balestrieri. The Baldasserona car park, which is most easily accessed by the road from Rimini, is easily extended with minimal environmental impact on the landscape, while the Piazza Borghesi is located in an area of the city centre which is not overloaded with trade establishments and which also provides several alternative access routes to the tourist areas. The length of the ascent route allows for a number of intermediate exits at well-spaced strategic points. An underground excavation is connected by a mixed circulation system of escalators, moving walkways and elevators.

The second scheme connects the sports ground overlooking the Strada Sottomontana to the Cava Antica, which is at present used as a car park. With careful landscaping, the sports ground could become a coach park for 20 coaches, providing a drop-off point and vertical access via the slope of the Rupe del Titano. The ascent system of two slanting lifts with two-storey cars would be invisible from the square. The Cava Antica would become a well-designed pedestrian space adjacent to the old city core.

OPPOSITE: Site plan; ABOVE, L TO R: Scheme 1 – perspective; section; BELOW: Scheme 2 – perspective; section

VILLA

Fregene Seaside, Italy

With A D'Addario, S Lombardozzi
and M Mondello

*The site overlooks a coast road which divides
the property from the beach. The basic typological idea derives from the need to provide
the dining and living room area with a view of
the sea. This would have been impossible to
achieve with a traditional arrangement of living
space downstairs and bedrooms upstairs. So
the arrangement was inverted: the public
areas of the house are related directly to the
landscape, with care being taken to avoid the
unnatural and vague look of raised buildings
(eg buildings on pilotis, or the rural houses
typical of reclaimed areas, which have a
cattle-shed on the ground floor and stairs
leading to a dwelling above). A small amount
of earthwork allows the incongruity to be easily
solved without any reduction in the functionality
of the house.*

*The bedrooms on the ground floor open on
to a 'secret garden' with trees and a swimming
pool, sheltered from the noise of the traffic and
the beach; whereas the living area, veranda
and attic, set at the top of the small artificial
hill, between the site boundary and the curved
stone wall, find the right relationship with the
horizon, visually 'jumping' over the street and
the beach complexes.*

*The strict regulations governing the conser-
vation of the landscape and the client's requirements (a covered surface of 75 square
metres), have practically prescribed the
building volume. Materials have been chosen
to withstand climatic corrosion: a curved dry
stone retaining wall in limestone, external walls
coated with vitreous mosaic tiles; window and
door frames in natural anodised aluminium;
the copper roof. The villa pays homage to the
architecture of José Antonio Coderch and
Luigi Moretti.*

*OPPOSITE, FROM ABOVE, L TO R: Front elevation;
rear elevation; side elevation; second level plan;
FROM ABOVE, L TO R: Perspective; axonometric;
longitudinal section; site plan; axonometric*

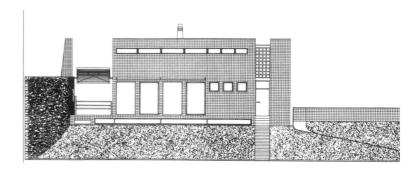

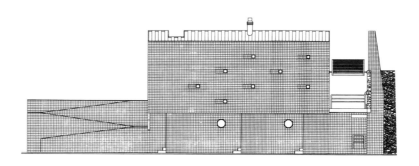

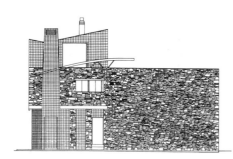

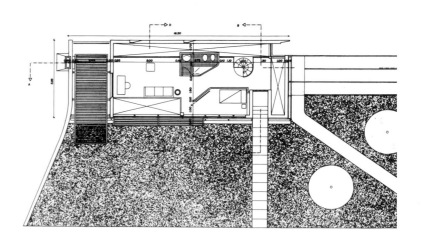

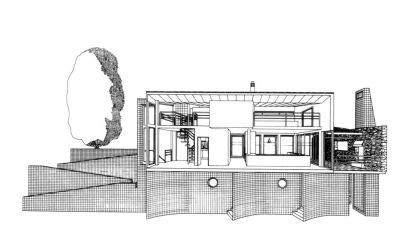

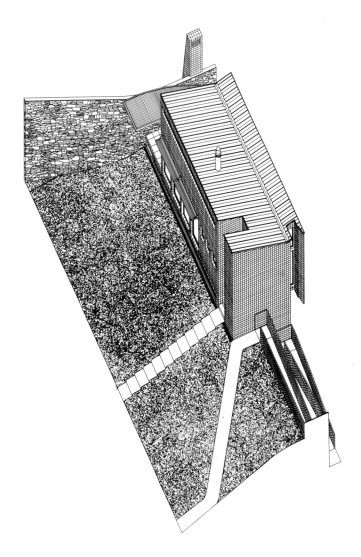

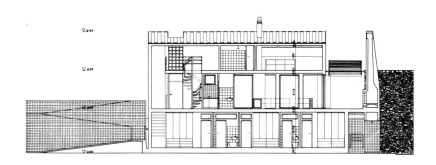

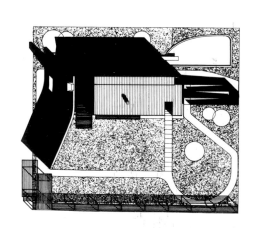

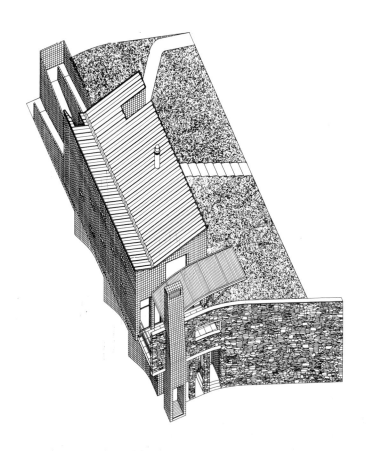

ITALY

CDS ASSOCIATES

Born in Naples, Antonio Costa graduated with honours from the Faculty of Architecture, Naples, in 1984. He started his own practice, taking part in the restoration of some ancient Neapolitan monasteries (S Pietro Martire and SS Apostoli) and designing residential interiors. Giancarlo Scognamiglio, also born in Naples, gained an honours degree at the same university, in 1982 . He worked with Professor Salvatore Bisogni, both as assistant on his course at the university, and in practice, designing residential buildings and a nursery school.

In 1987 Costa and Scognamiglio began their own joint practice, called CDS Associates. It was the beginning of a partnership, which has not only distinguished itself on the Neapolitan architectural scene by the novelty of its language, but also completed a wide variety of projects and achieved some notable successes in less than ten years. In this time they have built four important restaurants for McDonald's in southern Italy (Naples, Pompei, Salerno, Taranto), four small bank agencies (Naples, Avellino, Crotone, Torre Orsaia) and the offices of a Neapolitan bank; restored farming centres along the coast in Campania (Pozzuoli, Massalubrense, Sant'Agata) and an industrial building in Naples; redesigned a tourist village (Ischia); and developed the project for the extension of the S Paolo stadium in Naples. They have also completed many small projects in Naples, such as the design of a painting exhibition in the Royal Palace of Naples, the Benetton Atelier and a number of other shops. They have participated in several national and international competitions (for schools, sports centres, public buildings, Europan 3).

In particular, the conversion of traditional cinemas into multi-screen halls has given CDS Associates the opportunity to develop their own expressive autonomy. The practice has realised new spaces in many towns in southern Italy (the Modernissimo cinemas in Naples and Salerno, the Carmen cinema in Mirabella

Eclano, the America in Naples, the project for the multimedia hall in Cava dei Tirreni). The Naples Modernissimo has been published in important Italian architectural reviews (*L'Arca*, *Ventre*, *Tracce di architettura*).

CDS Associates are a young practice, with a realistic conception of the architectural discipline. Their architecture is not based on theory, but on craft, deriving strength from the search for quality and the basic values of construction. Their work, as an authentic expression of a contemporary vision, is centred on the question of space, and aims for an expressive clarity built upon a correspondence between form and content. Their experience offers a practical understanding of materials, specifications, methods of construction and ways of integrating structures and services with architecture.

Recently they have developed computerised systems to refine their design methods and monitor job progress, resources and profitability.

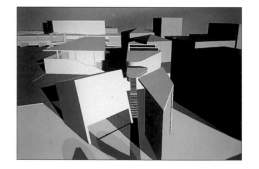

CIVIC CENTRE

Quarrata (Pistoia), Italy

Europan 3 Competition 1993

The project occupies the central area of the town, which is of no particular interest or architectural quality. New commercial spaces, public buildings, residences and offices are intended to give the site its own urban identity.

The main approach has been to conceive of the architectural project as having the capacity to describe reality, according to a less ideological vision, and with the aim of understanding and satisfying human 'reasons' and needs. Thus the design does not define a static space; on the contrary, it arranges some volumes according to a dynamic balance. The organisation of the plan aims to create both large and small spaces with different, contemporary uses and functions.

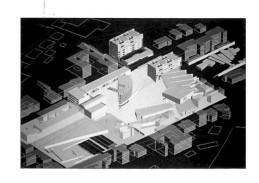

FROM ABOVE: Computer-generated perspectives; model visualisation; OPPOSITE: Site plan; Axonometric; RIGHT, FROM ABOVE: Computer generated perspectives

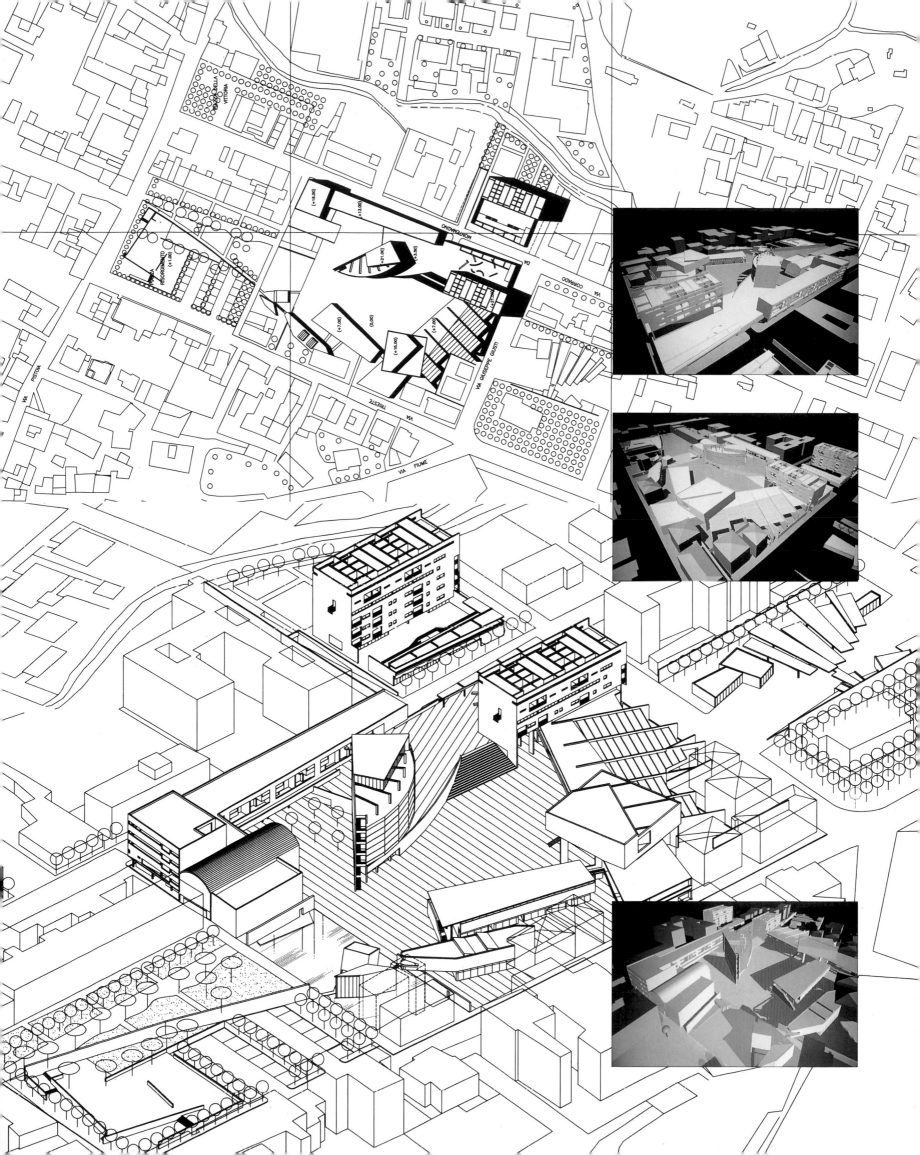

MODERNISSIMO CINEMA

Naples, Italy

The conversion of an old cinema into a new four-screen cinema required particular attention to the existing structure and context – the ancient heart of Naples.

The juxtaposition of the volumes of the four auditoriums and the organisation of the public spaces both derive from attempts to use the frame of the existing building, with the intention of preserving its shell. The public spaces are connected by a steel staircase, which seems to hang in the triple-height void.

The particularity of the project has allowed a deep exploration of differences in simple and apparent realities – materials, colours, space and light. The elegance of this work stems from its simplicity: nothing is redundant, and the form of each element is related to its function.

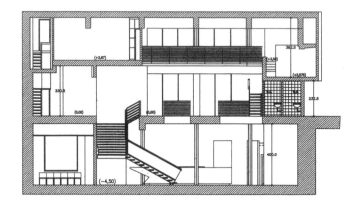

FROM ABOVE: Cross-section; longitudinal section; upper level plan; ground level plan

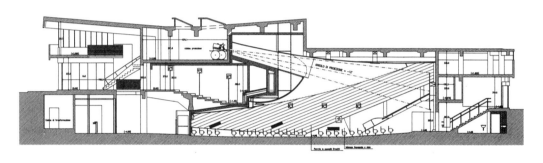

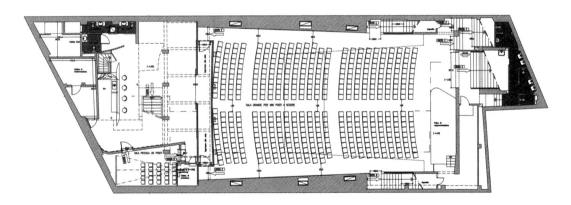

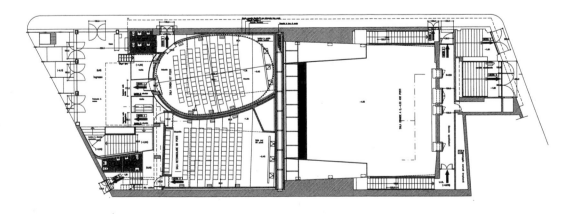

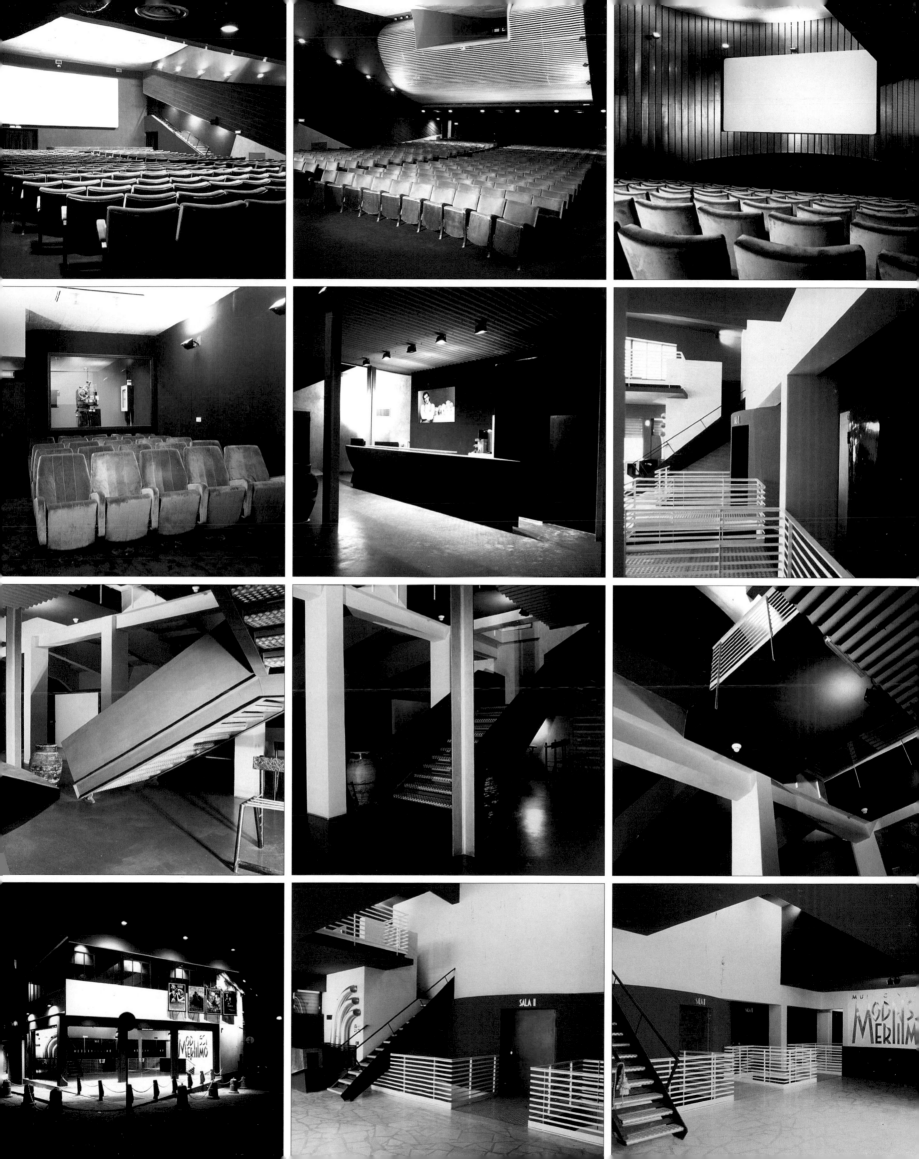

JAPAN

MIKAN

Mikan (the Group of the Tangerine) was formed in 1995. The partners are Kiwako Kamo, Yosuke Kumakura, Masashi Sogabe, Masayoshi Takeuchi, Manuel Tardits and several Mac computers. The group has a 'soft' structure within which each of the partners moves freely between projects.

A few hints to grasp reality:

The eyes of the child: no clear strategy, no clear image and no clear definition but the eyes of a beginner. When you look at a landscape, at a programme, at an urban situation, at a building, you try to see it with the clearest mind. No white, no black, just a grey.

On the importance of being earnest: 'What is well thought out is expressed clearly and the words for communication come easily'. The architect is a dictator by essence, but architecture does not have to dictate anything. It pre-exists in our minds and on our Mac screens prior to contact with the real world, but it exists because of and for the people. We do not change the world, we accept it and add a few touches.

Banal, vulgar and strange: architecture is not beautiful and reality is not dirty. Quoting Garciá Márquez, one can speak of 'the strange poetic quality of everyday life'. Try a recipe: place vernacular examples, advertisements and masterpieces in a pan. Add understatement and literality, mix and cook, serve when ready.

Renewal of New Realism or 'the serene evidence of the serial refrigerator': a refrigerator is as delicate and mysterious as the Alhambra. A television screen, a novel, certainly brings as much reality and space as the Parthenon or Katsura.

Context is not to be taken literally and things are always full of depth.

NHK BROADCAST STATION

Nagano, Japan

The new NHK station is a permanent facility of 6,000 square metres, which will be built for the next Winter Olympic Games in Nagano in 1998. There are four guiding principles for the scheme.

The functional iceberg: the three zones of the programme are superimposed. The studios, their facilities and the technical room are underground. The public space is on the ground level, and administration offices occupy the upper floors.

The public space: the public area is linked to a huge square. A screen of pilotis and a courtyard define the thresholds of public and private space. Above the studios, a suspended garden allows people to enjoy the panorama of the mountains, and to experience the building as part of a larger landscape.

The urban front: the bare facade of aluminium louvres and an inner facade on the ground level, the 'Information Wall' formed by the protruding volume of the studios, delimit the square. The wall is an interactive element which displays television screens, computer monitors and windows to the studios.

The monolith: to achieve the urban front, the antenna tower extends the whole building vertically to face the square. The tower becomes part of the whole. It is multi-functional: a structural device supporting the antennas, a sign and a didactic space which reveals the multiple layers of the iceberg.

BELOW: Section; plan; OPPOSITE: Model views

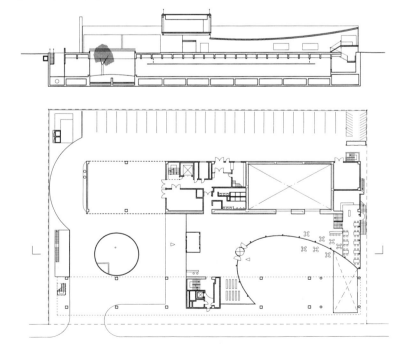

SHOPPING CENTRE

Yatsushiro, Japan

This project stands on a large flat site located in an agricultural and suburban area of a medium-sized town in southern Japan. It consists of a large store of 10,000 square metres and small independent shops and restaurants of 5,000 square metres. Two principles guide the scheme.

The grid: the site divides into several areas, between which remain isolated private houses. In order to unite these different elements, an abstract organising grid was set up. The grid separates different zones of changing functions, according to periods of time and space requirements. No distinct separation is intended between buildings and outdoor space, instead a spatial continuum of the grid is achieved.

Showcases and billboards: the buildings are bare, transparent boxes without strong identity. They look like banal containers or simple showcases for the goods. The whole scheme is also covered with billboards and banners, for information and advertisements.

BELOW: Site and roof plan; ground level plan; RIGHT: Model views; OPPOSITE, FROM ABOVE: East-west sections; north-south sections; model views

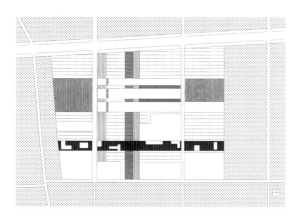

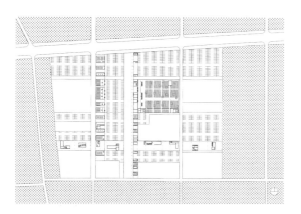

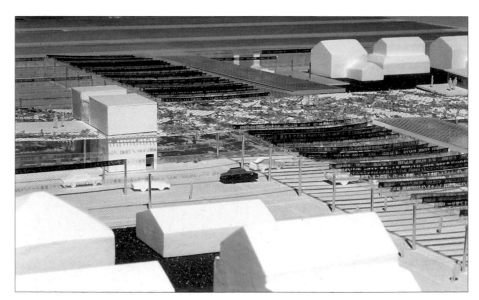

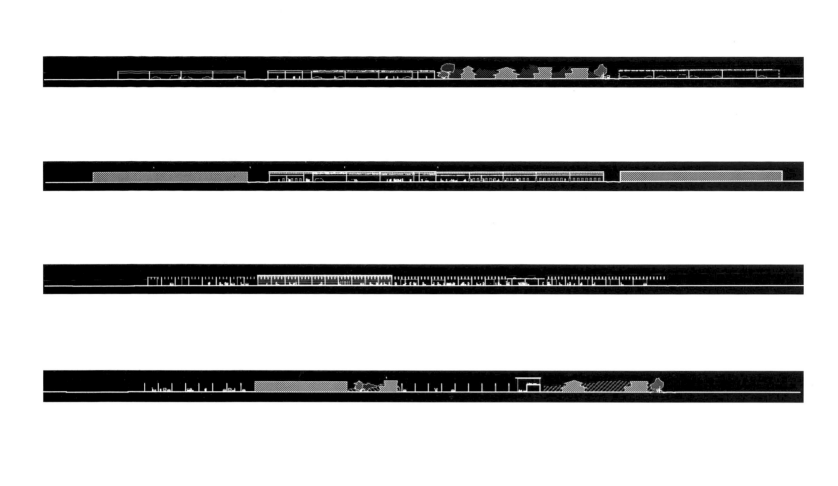

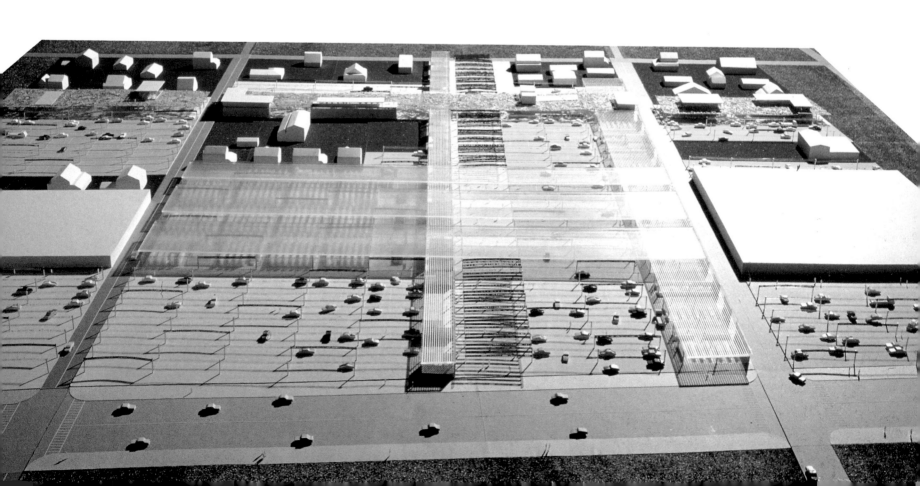

JAPAN

WORKSTATION
Akiko & Hiroshi Takahashi

Thoughts on Architectural Form

In today's society of excessive consumption, a myriad of images are consumed every day. Architectural form is no exception. Even projects that are not explicitly designed to promote a specific image are instantly classified according to the vast lexicon of architectural forms. Whether the designers like it or not, their work is labelled with a given image, and thus forms are tied to images in order to be consumed as 'information'.

For many centuries, architecture has been a vehicle for impressive imagery and, as the shifting trends in facade fashions show, buildings have long been 'consumed' in this way. The current situation is different only in the sense that the speed of consumption has increased relentlessly. Moreover, the veritable flood of styles also makes it much more difficult to feel the forces of the building form as architecture.

Today, we are gradually liberating ourselves from the psychological prohibitions and fetters of Modernism. On the other hand, the diversity of meaning and the goals are becoming more and more ambiguous. We all face the problem of losing sight of our position in the world. There is no longer a place for a universally valid methodology or 'ism'. From now on, only individual solutions are acceptable. Nevertheless, the fundamental question remains as to what we should use as a foundation.

Reflecting today's conditions, facades are completely covered with inorganic patterns; eliminated as faceless, transparent surfaces; or turned completely into media as screens for the projection of advertising and other imagery. Increasingly, attempts are being made to make architecture more 'common'.

We intend not to simplify the building forms following Minimalism, but to make clear responses through the composition of simple geometric shapes set against the various internal and external conditions or aspects of the buildings. We

believe that our completed projects should be open to various unexpected readings. We seek ways and means to make 'open' spaces that, while composed of clear shapes, are not restricted by them. In order to realise this, we intend to design open-ended structures or compositions with a primary geometry that never unifies the building into a uniform whole. In other words, we try to endow every part of the building with a distinct identity and compose an architecture as an efficient assemblage of parts. For example, the exterior appearance of the Sakamoto Ryoma Memorial Hall is a three-dimensional composition of several divergent volumes. At the Nakamachidai Community Center, the abstract quality of space is derivative of the application of parts, every one of which insists on its distinct presence through its material, colours and structural system. In this project, instead of diminishing the role structural elements play in the process of abstraction, we treat them as forms that are powerful, but not rigid. Consequently, materials, colours and structural elements play equal roles in generating architectural form.

The Osawano Health Care and Welfare Center project is another experiment in this direction. The building is 150 metres long, defined by a series of slightly modulated sectional shapes; the three dimensionality of the overall form is increased by the sequential alteration of the steel frames and their undulating disposition. This arrangement provides a degree of freedom in designing various size rooms and also assures a simple and distinct outline for the complex facility.

In short, we always strive to arrive at clear shapes or abstract form, to create composition through the amplification of the various aspects and conditions of each project and, as far as possible, to eliminate the massiveness and monumentality with which large buildings are normally identified.

NAKAMACHIDAI COMMUNITY CENTER
Kumamoto, Kyushu, Japan

This district centre fulfils the everyday needs of the local residents, consisting of a gymnasium and other spaces used for a variety of purposes. Our initial design approach was two-fold: first, we wished to provide an effective open space on a site which was both small and contextually complex; second, we wanted to make the gymnasium a positive part of the overall composition.

A circular forecourt has been created in the north-west part of the site, between the building itself and the housing along the main road. The half-mirrored glass, which wraps the forecourt facade, fragments the reflected scenery into vertical strips.

The gymnasium, located on the railway side, is linked visually to the lobby-like corridor at second floor level. A curved void is formed between the circular wall, which defines one side of this corridor, and the arc of the curtain wall, which bounds the forecourt. In contrast to the external space, the flow of space and people around this curved void provides a continuous spatial experience. The V-shaped steel columns, which carry the vertical loads of the crescent-shaped space, and the roofslab, which correspondingly alternates in thickness to the flow of loads, serve to express the idea of a place which is itself in a state of flux.

OPPOSITE, FROM ABOVE: Second floor plan; first floor plan; isometric

OSAWANO HEALTH CARE AND WELFARE CENTER

Osawano, Japan

This multi-purpose facility, which benefits from a hot spring on the site, is intended to provide an opportunity for health and welfare activities. It consists of a daycare facility for the aged, a number of rooms for activities, study rooms, a pool and hot spring complex, and a communal hall.

The site is near the River Jintsu, at the point where the river valley opens onto the plain at the centre of the town. The building is a long, thin structure, stretching across the full width of the site which lies parallel to the river.

The building depth gently changes along the undulating plain, providing a shift in expression. In elevation, the building is divided into a frame-like upper section and a wall-like lower section. The use of a continuous V-shaped frame for the upper section helps to reduce any sense of bulkiness. The frame is glazed where necessary to form interior spaces.

The basic composition of the building has been derived from a sense of location and the activities to take place within the facility. People approaching the building can sense the presence of the river, even if they cannot see it, due to the receding line of mountains each side of the valley. The design reinforces this subtle perception.

The form of the building comprises a simple, continuous section, providing freedom in the planning of variously sized rooms, and a distinct silhouette for a complex building.

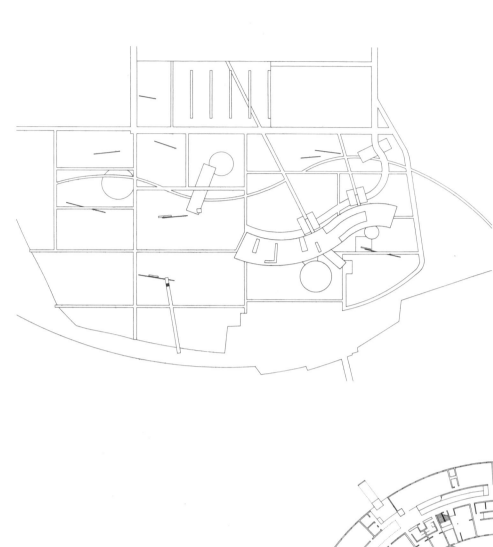

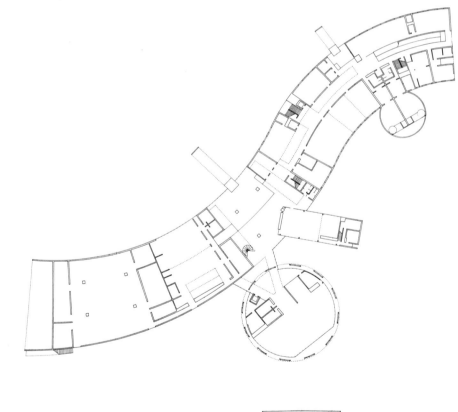

FROM ABOVE: Site plan; first floor plan; section; south elevation

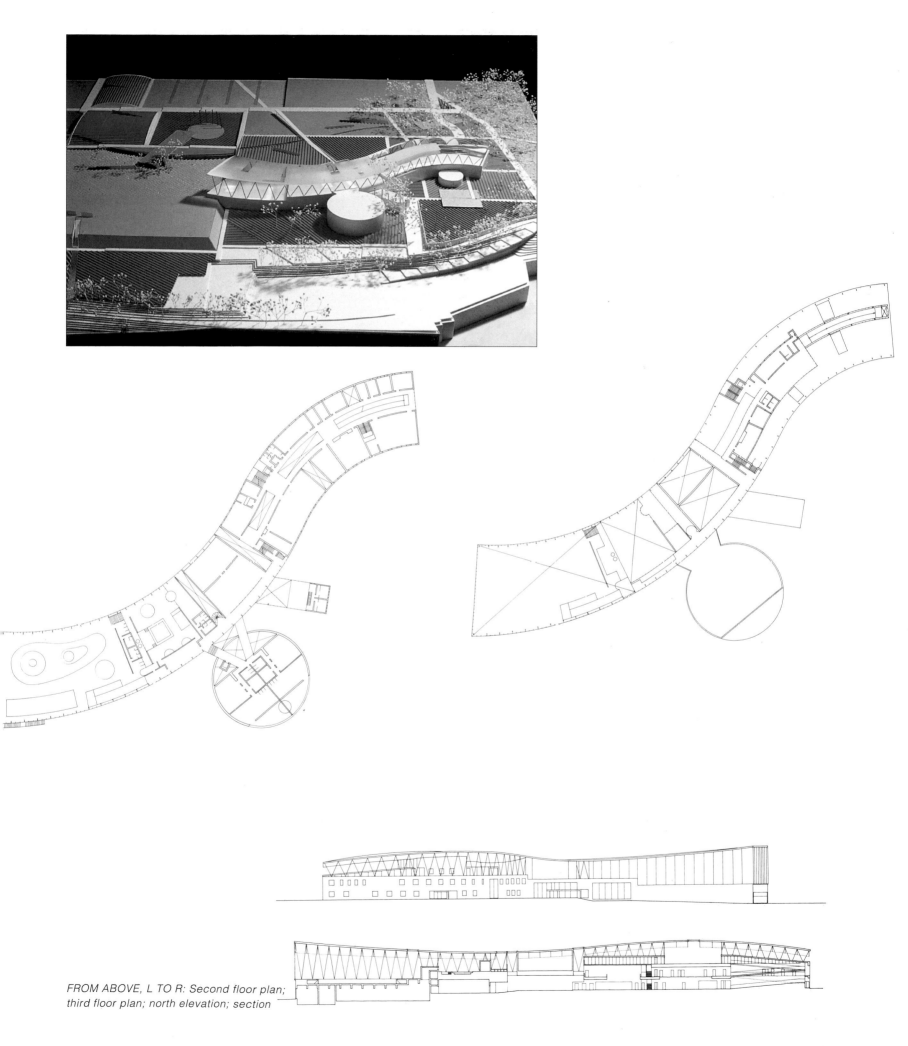

FROM ABOVE, L TO R: Second floor plan;
third floor plan; north elevation; section

THE NETHERLANDS

STUDIO 333

The critical question for architecture in the coming century may very well be a question of practice. Traditionally, the work of the architect has defined itself simply as the art of building. Yet, given such collective transformations as the collapse of the discrete object, the ever-increasing influences of different cultures, the convergences of not only multinational economic and political activity but also of new technological processes and combinations with the natural world, it seems unfathomable for architectural practice to continue as if nothing were happening.

As a studio, we find ourselves moving more and more away from merely representing the world in our work, choosing instead to form architectural and urban strategies to *operate* in that world. For us, the material integration of the social, the urban and the architectural pushes the design possibilities of architectural work, encouraging the invention of new forms, new modalities, new ways of thinking. In

that sense our practice is experimental and explorative; we seek nothing less than the investigation of higher forms of organisation and combinations, immersing architecture with contemporary cultural conditions: *the creation of new group form*.

Composed of an international team of collaborators, Studio 333 has wilfully entered this arena of integrative thought as a multi-disciplinary organisation. Currently based in Rotterdam, it started out in 1990 as a London-based collective formed to develop the winning entry to the international competition for the Revitalisation of Samarkand and to act as a forum for debate. The studio has since evolved into an open-based organisation which at the moment has four principal members: Burton Hamfelt, Christopher Moller, Dominic Papa and Jonathan Woodroffe. The organisation operates as a collective endeavour in which certain principals organise 'clusters' (sub-groups), to perform and execute various projects. Key professional collaborators

from various disciplines are involved from the beginning of the projects.

The work of Studio 333 can best be characterised as an attempt to chart and engage the changing conditions that define the contemporary city, and to explore of new urban forms and techniques for the city of the 21st century. Since 1991, the studio has lectured throughout Western and Eastern Europe. In 1992 it received a national design award for its proposal for the city of Karlsruhe, Germany, which included research with Ove Arup and Partners in the field of explorative and environmental design. In 1994 the studio was awarded the first prize in the Europan 3 competition for the Groningen site, The Netherlands, which is now being worked towards realisation. Recent work has included actively collaborating with civic municipalities in articulating sustainable urban strategies for Groningen and Zaanstad, The Netherlands.

THE ACTIVE MATRIX

Groningen, The Netherlands

Project team: Nicholas Barratt-Boyes, Burton Hamfelt, Stephen McDougall, Chris Moller, Dominic Papa, Emmanuelle Poggi, Lisa Raynes, Jonathan Woodroffe

Lying between the historic city centre and a 1930s residential district, the 100,000-square-metre site is at present a marginal zone, occupied by abandoned warehouses and car parks. In the original programme, housing units and other mixed functions were organised as components that were defined as 'attractors', 'condensers' and 'mediators' in order to intensify the site. The premise of these elements was not to organise space, but to act as catalysts to set in motion and link into larger existing processes. The intention has been to create a wild and dense urban tapestry, a three-dimensional stained-glass window: an environment where 'space' is used, in the words of Michel de Certeau, 'as a practised place'.

OPPOSITE: Perspective; FROM ABOVE, L TO R: Attractors, mediators, condensers and movement, ring analysis diagrams; model; perspectives

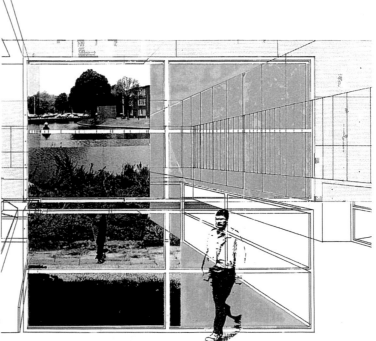

61

PRADO MUSEUM EXTENSION

Madrid, Spain

Project team: Burton Hamfelt, Erik Jensen,
Chris Moller, Stuart Mardeusz, Dominic Papa,
Jonathan Woodroffe

*Immersed within a rich dense foliage, the site
once settled only by the four Prado buildings
now embodies the spatial and temporal dignity
of the 'campus in the city'. However, at
2,000,000 people a year (and growing), 8,000
per day and 17 per minute, the Prado Museum
has reached the density levels of a small
international airport.*

*The brief required that the built component
be simply an attached volume at the back of
the main building, the Villanueva. This project
instead offers an alternative solution in the
form of an infrastructural strategy that responds to this growth, acting as a multi-spined
organ, feeding and linking the museum into a
pastoral complex, where sectionally varied
spaces curl, split and open their membranes
to maximise connections, light and views.*

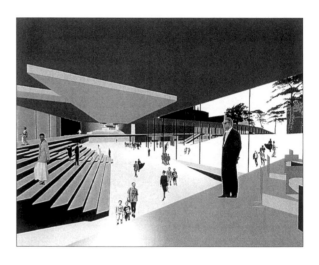

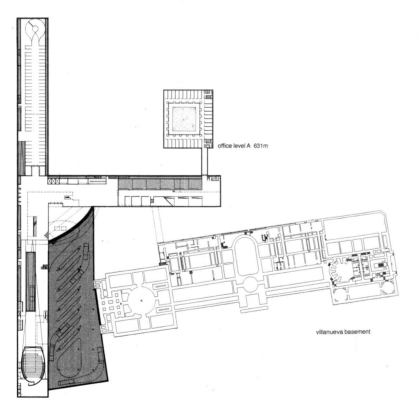

office level A 631m

villanueva basement

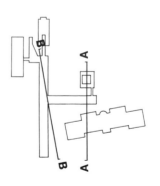

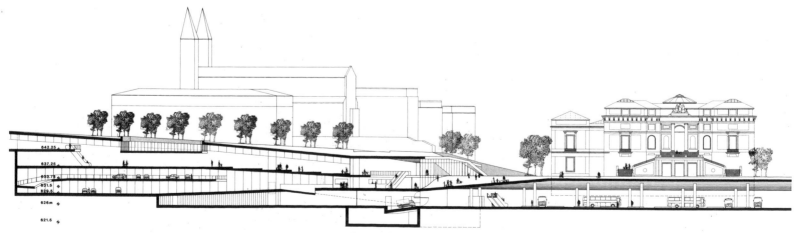

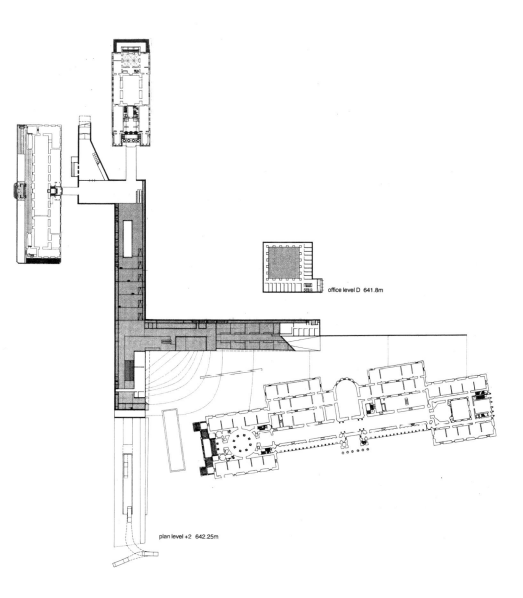

office level D 641.8m

plan level +2 642.25m

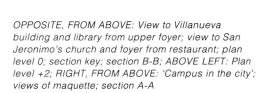

OPPOSITE, FROM ABOVE: View to Villanueva
building and library from upper foyer; view to San
Jeronimo's church and foyer from restaurant; plan
level 0; section key; section B-B; ABOVE LEFT: Plan
level +2; RIGHT, FROM ABOVE: 'Campus in the city';
views of maquette; section A-A

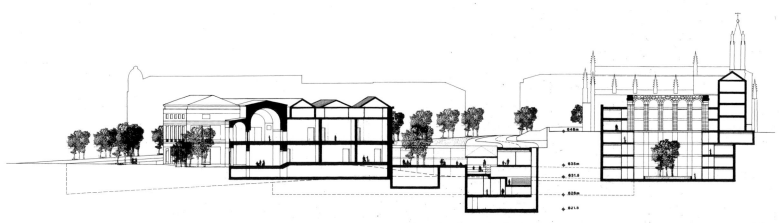

THE NETHERLANDS

RENE VAN ZUUK

In 1988 I completed my studies at the Technical University of Eindhoven, The Netherlands. My course speciality was building production technology rather than architecture.

For me, as an architect, it is essential to know how the details of a building are made, because once you have that knowledge you can make anything you want. Until now most of my buildings have been objects. Free-standing elements. All of these elements are strong forms which, in my view, best present the essence of the function and atmosphere of their surroundings. I make use of several architectural ingredients to achieve these strong forms; structure, the combination of materials, texture, technique, and last but not least, form associations.

All of my designs are made as models. I rarely draw. Many models are built, from the first idea to the last detail. Working in this way allows me to show the client what is possible within the forms, even from an early stage in the design process.

After completing my studies I worked for Skidmore, Owings and Merrill in London and Chicago. In 1989 I won the competition for my house Psyche. It took me two years to find enough sponsors for this project, and another year to build it.

I started my own one-man practice in Almere in 1993 after Psyche was built. The kinds of projects and commissions I get varies from little bridges to developers' housing schemes, from sculpture to a soccer training centre for Ajax. If the project becomes too big for me to handle alone, as is the case with the project for Ajax, I make use of an architectural support office which takes care of all of the non-design aspects of the project.

CANAL SERVICE HOUSE,

Easterlock, Groningen, The Netherlands

The service house by the Easterlock in Groningen was commissioned by the province of Groningen as part of a major restructuring plan for the Van Starkenborg Canal. The area around the lock is open and is approximately 80,000 square metres. One of the conditions set down by the city planners of Groningen was that the building should have a presence in the vast emptiness of its surroundings.

A 200-square-metre service house was required. The front of the house had to be within 1.5 metres from the side of the lock but due to the structure of the lock, the base could be no less than 6.5 metres above the lock. The

lock serviceman and most of the other personnel work in one room.

The ground floor and the first floor are rather small and the functions are secondary. The principal floor is the second floor, where all of the daily personnel work together in one small main room. From this floor there is a marvellous view from the front over the Van Starkenborg Canal. There are no windows to the rear of this room, as the service house also controls four bridges in the canal. The form of the service house is mainly functional, but it also has features of old Dutch sailing ships and the eyes of an insect.

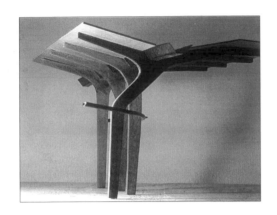

PSYCHE

Almere, The Netherlands

In 1989 a competition was held to design an unusual house on an allotment in Almere. Psyche was awarded the first prize and therefore could be built. The site is quite beautiful. There is a small lake to the front of the house and a canal and open area to the rear. The first-floor living room is designed to give a beautiful 360-degree panorama of the picturesque scenery of the area.

The entrance on the ground floor leads into a large double-height hall. The kitchen is located in the hall and the two bedrooms and bathroom are adjacent to the hall.

The house has two structural systems: the walls and the first floor are carried by a steel structure of tubes, and the roof is carried by four organically formed steel trees. The trunks of the trees describe a circle segment in such a way that they seem to be performing a ballet.

SPAIN

ENRIC MASSIP i BOSCH
Estudi d'arquitectura

Our practice tries to keep its structure to a minimum. At present an average number of three to four people work in our office. Whenever possible, all aspects of a project – structure calculation, construction details, and so on – are developed by us in order to keep total control of the design. Nevertheless, occasional partnerships or collaborations with external professionals are established when necessary.

Our main subject so far has been the design of private houses, both new and renovated. Other projects include public works such as sports facilities and social housing, as well as commercial and industrial interiors.

We believe that the material qualities of architecture contain the means to create immaterial perceptions. Architecture can only be experienced by inhabiting its built spaces. Thus, construction is quintessential to architecture, the *sine qua non* for the display of all its qualities.

We attempt to achieve significant spaces that possess qualities such as calmness, stillness and clarity, but that none the less produce a sense of mystery and expectation, like suspended moments in time. Proportions, materials and visual/spatial relationships are used to convey these feelings inside these spaces. On the other hand, we consider that the existence of the building should maintain an equal relation with the environment: be part of it by being within it. Devices such as camouflage or domination should be reserved for very specific situations.

Our present research focuses on the (re)organisation of the domestic space: this is for us the field in which architecture will test its basic *raison d'être* in the coming years, and so is worthy of any effort we can make.

CA – CASA TÍ i CIÓ

Falset (Tarragona), Catalonia

The house stands at the end of a row of detached houses. Regulations demanded a significant setback from the boundaries that limited the buildable area even more. In order to keep as much as possible of the plot free, a multi-level house was chosen. A relation with the surroundings is achieved by projecting elements from the original solid; porches, dry-stone walls or volumes. The ground floor has no partitions and is open to the garden, whereas the upper floor is enclosed by partitions and lit by skylights. The construction method improves on traditional masonry techniques by incorporating such novelties as an interior bearing wall, projected insulation, and an exterior plastered curtain wall creating a ventilated cavity wall.

LEFT: Ground level plan; RIGHT, FROM ABOVE: East elevation; west elevation

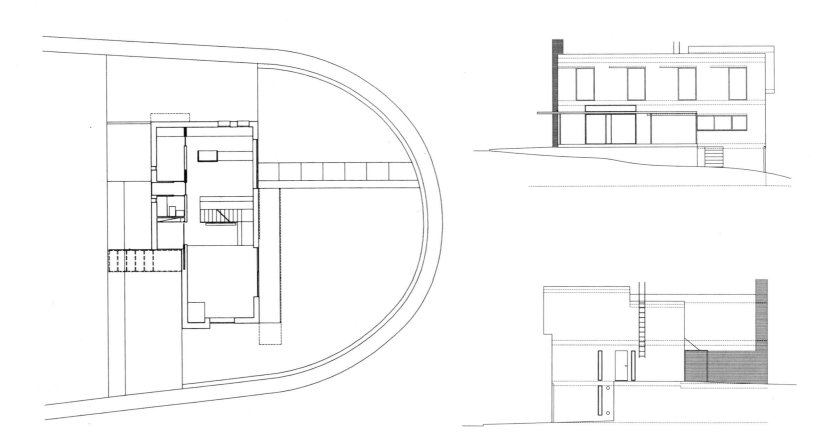

68

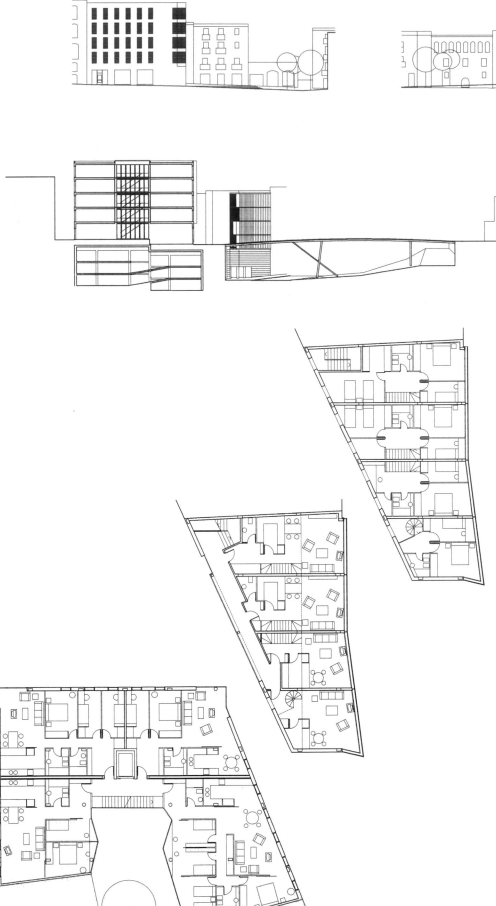

QH – PUBLIC HOUSING AND URBAN RENEWAL

Manresa (Barcelona), Catalonia, with Joan Sabaté and Horacio Espeche, architects

This prize-winning project proposal had two purposes: to define a project that could become a model for the renewal of the old centre of Manresa, establishing an approach to scale, size, density and materials that could be generally applied; and to provide floor plans that went beyond the standard layouts encouraged by social housing regulations. Both the organisation of the floor plans and the sections reflect this approach.

To establish a relation with the pre-existing buildings, where regulations defined the proportions of fenestration, and to give an open relation with the exterior, we introduced light glass and wood galleries, with vernacular references to the surroundings. In some cases, these galleries generate a second interior circulation that renders the apartment richer in perceptual possibilities.

FROM ABOVE: Plaza elevations; section showing pedestrian bridge; upper level plan of maisonette apartment building; lower level plan of maisonette apartment building; typical plan of courtyard building; OPPOSITE LEFT, FROM ABOVE: Sections through parking; south-east elevation; site plan; OPPOSITE RIGHT, FROM ABOVE: Model; riverside view of model; photomontages

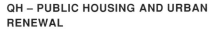

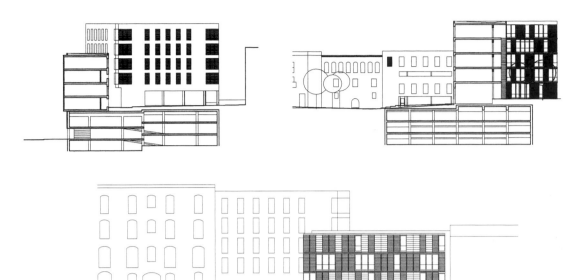

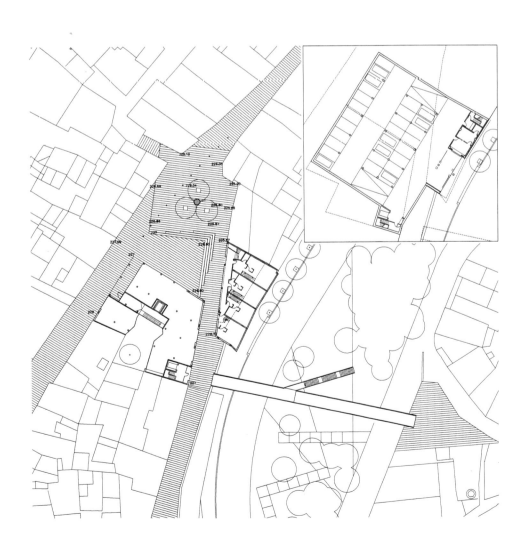

UNITED KINGDOM

FAT
Fashion Architecture Taste

Ideas have been traditionally propagated through the media of the exhibition and the manifesto. So, should this published work (and by implication, all published works of architecture) be viewed in this light? If so, what are we to conclude from the work produced to date by the architecture and fine art practice of Fashion Architecture Taste? Given the overt 'stylishness' of the work, are we to infer that it exhibits principles which might be of use to us? Or is it merely the whimsical and esoteric output of a group attempting to advertise themselves in this magazine, which is concurrently attempting to authenticate itself as *au courant* with current fashion trends?

Clearly, the inclusion of the word 'Fashion' in the group's title hints at a territory that architecture might occupy – a volatile, fast-moving, image-led territory, prone to quotation and parody, and lying outside the ghostly cloud that permanently hovers over that architectural project – the search for the authentic.

One effect of electronic graphic systems allied to the commercial forces operating on the production of buildings is that 'styling' has become an integral part of environmental design. But is it not refreshing to watch designers making a stand for particular aesthetic issues in an architectural culture which, although dominated by the visual, refuses to acknowledge this in its schools of architecture, continuing to promote tired arguments about the 'superior virtues' of the technical? And is there really any difference between, with its selling of a 'look', *The World of Interiors* and the apparently more authentically architectural *El Croquis*?

Such questions are raised by the overtly constructed aesthetics of Fat's work, and the practice's history of collaboration with graphic designers and fine artists, as well as engineers, accentuates this emphasis on the visual.

Putting aside the startling agility and sense of style of the computer renderings, it becomes clear what is central to their work: the image as a site of collisions of different taste regimes and different conceptual locations; the acceptance that the search for the authentic single concept is a futile undertaking in the late-20th century; and the notion that the aim of the architectural project is to filter, select, cut and paste from a selection of cultural sources, in order to produce new arrangements which, like a Tarantino movie, vibrate with references to the familiar. In each of their projects, whether the street-based actions (Work, Adsite, Home Ideals, Mod Cons) or the interiors, there is always something recognisable, from somewhere else within something quite new. So, the truncated Richard Wilson shed is glimpsed beyond the James Turrell, the glowing surface past the shimmering expanse of the stainless steel bar.

Is this kind of re-assembly more problematical when the sources of the collage are high rather than low culture? This would seem to me to be a new tactic presenting new difficulties (and new opportunities), which poses the question: what happens if you appropriate the work of an artist like Turrell who is clearly searching for the sublime and the authentic, into

circumstances that deny this as perhaps even possible at this time? What risks are taken in the adoption of this strategy? Any? Is the appropriated object turned into a parody of itself or a fashion sign?

But then risk is what design is all about, and the inversion of the traditional intent of collage, which was to configure the banal into the poetic, the re-arrangement of the codes of everyday life, and now, the placing of the lyrical against the ordinary to produce something else again, seems a dangerous if intriguing process. Nevertheless, in spite of their claims to the contrary, within the images of Fat, there lies an attempt to drag out of the confusion – the endless circulations of information, the paranoia of consumption, the constant shrieks of Buy-Me-Believe-in-Me – work that has some sort of (dare I say) integrity.
David Greene

ANTI-OEDIPAL HOUSE
Case Study, Milton Keynes

'They fuck you up, your mum and dad.'
Fat proposes an anti-oedipal idyll, a suburban house prototype that opposes that ubiquitous architectural machinery of oedipal repression: the typical family dwelling. This house separates the parents from the child, allowing each to indulge their own particular obsessions – the parents in the arch-Modernist glass house where they may fulfil their passion for dinner parties and obsessive cleanliness, and the child in the voluptuous 'masturbatorium', lounging free from the parental gaze.

BELOW, L TO R: East section; south section; OPPOSITE, FROM ABOVE: Model view; plans; north-east section; west section

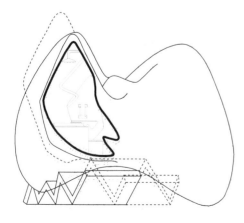

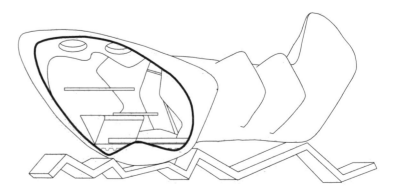

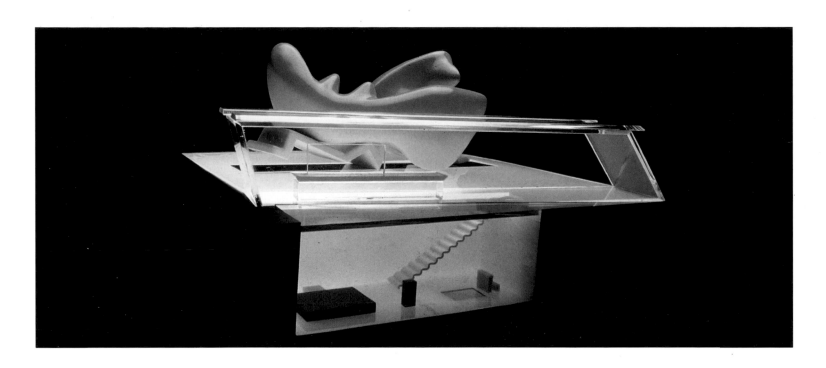

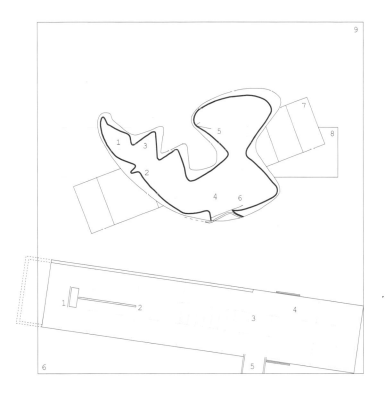

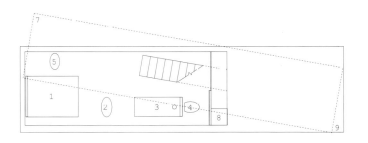

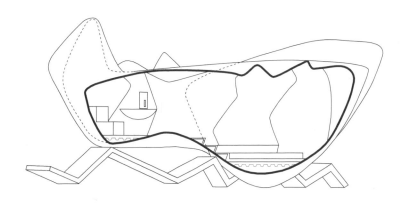

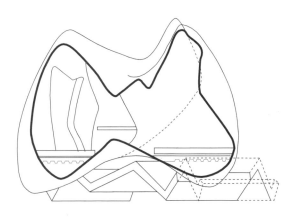

CHEZ GARSON

Conversion, London

A homage to Archigram's 'suburban sets' which examines the 'appropriation aesthetic' of modern day house-making, where image is deemed synonymous with lifestyle. A house within an ex-Baptist chapel indulges the clients' rural fantasies via the insertion of an interior barnyard facade. This allows the home owner to step in from a suburban north London street and enjoy the rustic experience of the great outdoors, complete with artificial sunlight.

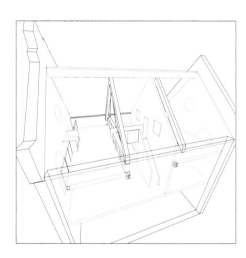

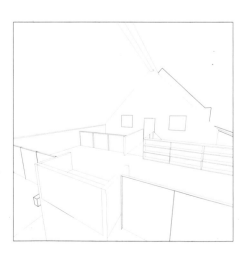

THE BRUNEL ROOMS

Leisure Complex, Swindon

Airports and allotments collide within an interior urbanism. Space is territorialised through the use of formally iconic objects suggesting disjunctive programmatic occupations. The familiar is reinvented by recodings and dislocations – a sprint down the running track starts by the glowing swimming pool, passes by baggage reclaim and breaks the tape in a suburban allotment. Lighting and servicing are requisitioned as spatial modulators – ambient neon lights are programmed to change colour and intensity over time and air-handling equipment is integrated experientially, creating cool zones responding to particular uses.

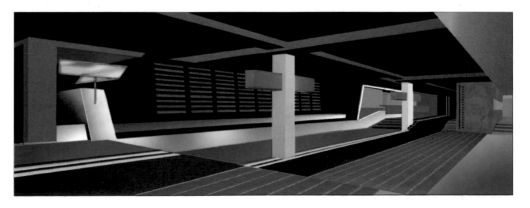

OPPOSITE, LEFT: Computer-generated perspectives; RIGHT: Computer-generated perspectives

UNITED KINGDOM

FOREIGN OFFICE ARCHITECTS

'Foreign' is defined as from outside; it attempts a definition by stating a position in space. Today, occupying a spatial position might be as important as adopting a political position was for the Modernist avant-garde. The production of vast amounts of information in the late-capitalist era has devalued representation as a vehicle of communication. Systems of signification, whether languages or value systems, are increasingly being replaced by material and spatial organisations as the basis of communication, exchange and consensus.

In the last seven years the map of the world has changed more than it did in the intervening years since the second world war. Whether they address the reunification of Germany, the break-up of the former Yugoslavia, the GATT Agreement, or the accord between Israel and Palestine on the Gaza Strip, negotiations are now concerned primarily with roads and rivers, connections to cities and seas. There is no more significant action than the production of space, no deeper meaning than a material organisation. Architecture no longer needs to embody concepts, symbols and ideologies. This is why we are interested in a *performative* approach to material practices, in which architecture is an artefact within a concrete assemblage rather than a device for *interpreting* or *signifying* material and spatial organisations. Ultimately, any action or form of knowledge is motivated by a desire to modify or create our environment, not to explain or signify it.

In their efforts to construct difference the movements that coincided with the onset of the late-capitalist era – historicism, regionalism, Deconstructivism – were essentially an escape from the rigidities of the Modernist, colonialist, enlightened project of universal rationality. But the fragmented spatial models produced by such movements are unable to account for the very fact that had produced them: the process of globalisation which originated in the need to disperse and absorb the over-accumulation of commodities. The other main concern of our research is the construction of a model which is capable of integrating differences into a coherent system. The problem is to discover how the spatial coherence which characterises globalised late-capitalist regimes can inform local differences, to approach the production of space as the articulation of *global* processes with *local* specificities, where global does not mean empty and local does not mean disconnected. As an architectural statement *after* Post-Modernism, *after* critical regionalism, *after* Deconstructivism, our strategy is to articulate the production of space which is coherently differentiated.

The Modernist techniques of erasure and homogenisation no longer seem appropriate as a way of achieving integration, nor is the identification of historical, regional and linguistic types or figures of any use in achieving differentiation – precisely because of their dependence on codes and systems of representation. We try to develop techniques that are capable of operating outside existing codes, to exploit the potential of a foreign operativity, to operate by migration, displacement, estrangement, not by seeking out origins or essences, developing genealogies, defining boundaries, assigning capacities or inventing languages. This is the origin of our interest in *de-territorialisation* and *re-territorialisation,* as processes in which specific domains and organisations are devoid of limits, origins, destination or significance: decoded, unbounded landscapes rather than overcoded, delimited places – and yet precise, specific, concrete.

A *nomadic* operativity does not imply a lack of control, but rather the development of specific modes of determination. Similarly, to engage in economic, social and urban processes of greater complexity does not imply an inability to determine, but an ability to become more sophisticated; to respond with complex orders rather than linear determinations, to redefine the limits of our control. The need for planning within material practices arises from the need to control the production of our environment. Any indeterminacy or inconsistency in the process is therefore simply the result of our lack of ability as planners.

YOKOHAMA INTERNATIONAL PORT TERMINAL

Yokohama, Japan

The concept of ni-wa-minato, suggesting a mediation between garden and harbour, was the starting-point of the project, which comprises a cruise passenger terminal and public spaces and facilities to be built on the Osanbashi pier. The artefact will operate as a mediating device between the two large social machines that make up the new institution: the system of public spaces of Yokohama and the cruise passenger flow, reacting against the rigid segmentation usually found in mechanisms dedicated to maintaining borders. The proposed structure will blur the borders between states, articulating differentially the various segments of the programme throughout a continuously varied form: from local citizen to foreign visitor, from flaneur to business traveller, from voyeur to exhibitionist, from performer to spectator.

Using the deformed and bifurcated ground surface to create a complementary public space to Yamashita Park, this proposal will result in the first perpendicular penetration of the urban space within Yokohama Bay.

The future YIPT allows for the boundaries between domestic and international to be shifted to cater for the traffic fluctuations. This demand for flexibility is not translated into a homogeneous space, but into a highly differentiated structure, a seamless milieu which allows for the broadest variety of scenarios: an ideal battlefield where the strategic position of a small number of elements will substantially affect the definition of the frontier, allowing the terminal to be occupied by locals or invaded by foreigners. The position of the urban leisure facilities at the end of the pier, combined with the organisation of the circulation as set of interlaced loops, turns the dead end of the pier into a public space.

The surface of the ground folds onto itself, forming creases that provide structural strength, like an origami construction. The classical segmentation between building-envelope and load-bearing structure disappears. The use of segmented elements such as columns, walls or floors has been avoided in favour of a move towards a materiality where the differentiation of structural stresses is not determined by coded elements but by singularities within a material continuum, more efficient against earthquake stresses.

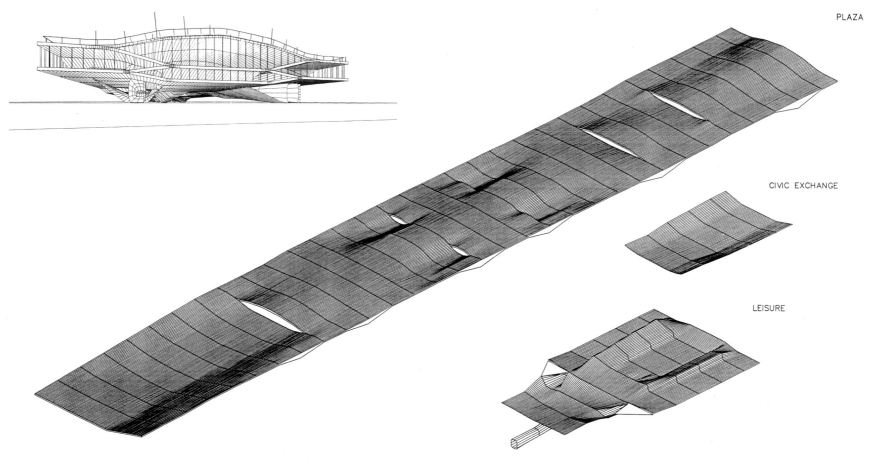

PLAZA

CIVIC EXCHANGE

LEISURE

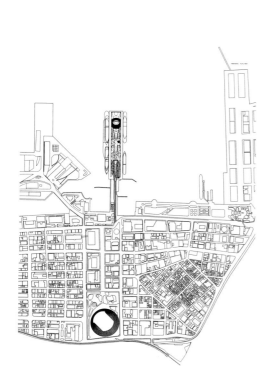

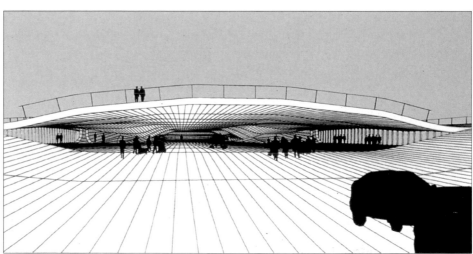

OPPOSITE LEFT, FROM ABOVE: View of sea approach; plaza; civic exchange; leisure; Port of Yokohama site plan; view of building from pier; entry to cruise terminal; bifurcation – cruise terminal/apron

RENOVATION OF THE MYEONG-DONG CATHEDRAL ENVIRONMENT

Seoul, Korea

The Myeong-Dong cathedral site in the heart of Seoul is not only the location and emblem of the Catholic Church in Korea, but also a symbol of democracy, as the location of the student riots against dictatorship. The competition brief asked for 35,000 square metres of programme, including office space, temporary residence, a convention and cultural centre for the Catholic Church, and the treatment of the public space of the complex.

The strategy was to integrate a very fragmented condition, programmatically and topographically. The proposal aims to con-

struct a public urban space in which all the different fragments will become unified: religious and political space, commercial and civic space; and to generate a topography able to accommodate large-scale public events. This would happen on two levels: on the surface of the plaza, and in the large sunken stadium, unifying the various parts of the programme into one single large space placed under the plaza.

The plaza, rising both to the south and to the east with a similar gradient, automatically produces a conic surface that can also be used as an open-air metropolitan auditorium for large-scale public events. Within that space, some topographical deformations of

the basic shape allow for access, light or structure, and diversify the quality of the space. Lightweight, temporary elements, can be placed within this space to provide further differentiated conditions.

The sunken stadium mirrors the mass events occurring on the surface of the plaza, and will provide the largest public space in central Seoul: an auditorium able to host an event for 11,000 spectators, or alternatively a series of multi-purpose auditoriums for simultaneous functions. This large facility is provided with retractable seating and folding vertical divisions, to allow reduction or expansion of the auditorium spaces.

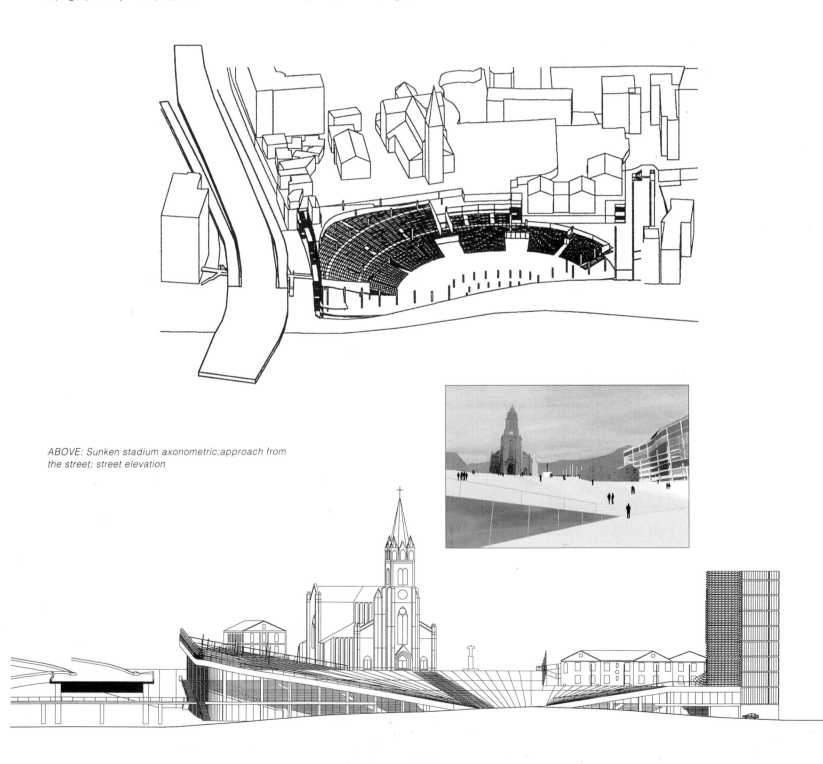

ABOVE: Sunken stadium axonometric; approach from the street; street elevation

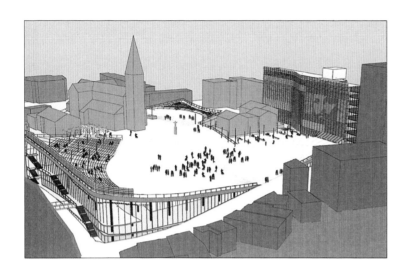

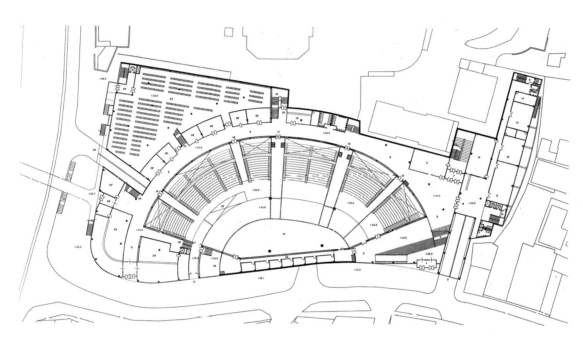

FROM ABOVE, L TO R: View of plaza; view from elevated highway; sunken stadium level plan; entry to civic facilities and approach to plaza

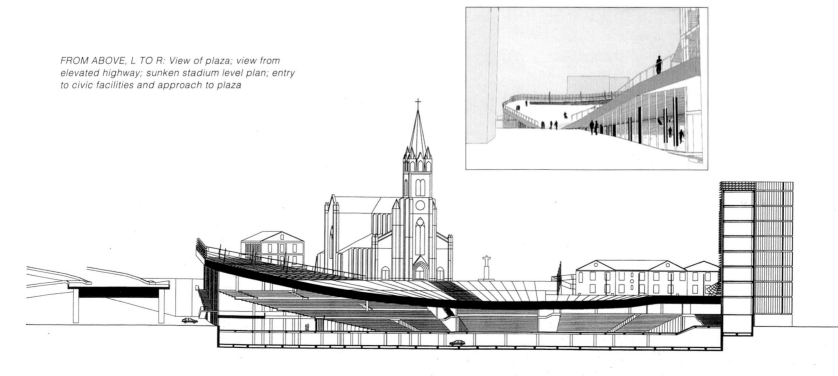

MUF

The disciplines of art and architecture converge in the collaboration of Muf. Illustrated are two independently completed projects, a gymnasium (1992) and an installation (1993), and the projects for the Museum of Women's Art and 'Purity and Tolerance' at the Architecture Foundation undertaken as Muf. At present Muf are working on an urban proposal for Southwark which slips the limit between public highway and private interior for Southwark Street and Bankside.

The Gymnasium, Waterloo, was designed by Juliet Bidgood Liza Fior Architects. Behind the mirrored end wall of the gymnasium lie the changing rooms and showers; they are arranged on two levels, women above, men below. In the women's changing room she stands naked, invisible to the gymnasium floor below, but able to survey that scene through a tilted transparent panel on her side of the mirrored wall. The availability of the unclothed women is reversed by this wall, which returns to her both the pleasure of nakedness and the pleasure of looking.

'Innerside' was an installation at the Architectural Association by Katherine Clarke. The horse comes down from its traditional place in the painting above the fireplace and is caught in the frame of the photograph as evidence of his now absent presence. The image has a contradictory status, it is simultaneously transparent and opaque, it covers over the scene it also shows, and similarly the pleasure of looking is caught between certainty and disbelief.

Muf work to blur and dissolve the conventions and categorical descriptions which limit architectural design. The collaborative constitution of the practice itself challenges professional demarcations, which are further disturbed by procedures of consultation that effectively acknowledge the interdependence of the producer and user of spaces. The spaces of the city are subject to diverse uses, desires and experiences: in urban design and public building Muf use the conventions of planning and zoning not to prescribe the limits of a situation, but to identify these diverse and shifting overlaps of desire and intention. The practice's design strategy incorporates these interplays and mediates interdependencies to produce places and spaces where one situation always includes the possibility of another. For example, a proposal that acknowledges the presence of the child, also includes the adult returned to the realm of the child, and access here becomes the norm, not a concession.

Embedded in the architect's drawn line and modelled form is the invisible reiteration of the architect's duty to know already all there is to know of a situation. Similarly, the conventions of architectural representation themselves describe potential spaces as if they are almost already built. The intention is a design process that can remain open to negotiation, and a design notation and language that include both the specific, the familiar and the strategic. For example, in the MWA conceptual design model, the kitchen table that has stood in for a woman's study and studio was taken as a model of simultaneous and multiple activity, able to invert and unfold the contained and linear typology of the 19th-century museum. The design strategy finds a resolution in materials and forms which give a spatial experience that is open to interpretation and use rather than fixed and given. In 'Purity and Tolerance' – the MWA fragment – the stretched ceiling has an ambivalence of edge and boundary, of excess and containment, experienced both as a threat and a pleasure.

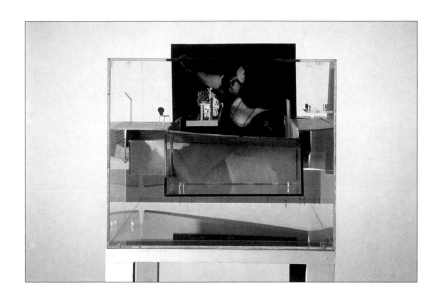

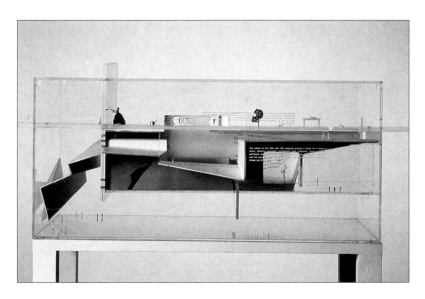

MUSEUM OF WOMEN'S ART

The design strategy for the MWA is to reveal the paradox inherent in opening up a hidden canon of work, only to enclose it again within the very institution that excluded it in the first place. In advance of a secured site, the model serves as a framework for consultation to develop the strategy and extend the ambitions of the client.

The model lays out potential relationships, interplays and interdependencies. The perspex box, which normally keeps dust off the model within, is cut and folded out to disclose the potential relationships within and around the proposed building; the museum interior opens out to the neighbourhood and street, minor misuse is included alongside the means to remain, the historic canon alongside contemporary work; the inclusion of the child as visitor, and the viewer themselves, in all their diversity, are revealed as legitimate subjects of another's gaze. These adjacencies and proximities allow for spatial design to disclose the social, political and historic conditions of women from the History of Art.

These issues of exclusion were developed at a scale of 1:1 in the installation 'Purity and Tolerance' with Katherine Shonfield. A glossy reflective stretch ceiling was installed in the exhibition space of the Architecture Foundation. From the raised part of the gallery and from the street, a view between the pristine edge of the latex and the mess of the existing surface above is disclosed. The assumed neutral perfection of the space of exhibition is reflected back by the ceiling fabric, this perfection is distorted by a restrained bulge of excluded liquid which threatens to pour in and ruin the space. The contradictory qualities of perfection and distortion, high reflection, great strength and fluid malleability is achieved by the titanium content of the latex. The titanium makes the material extremely pliable and the ceiling responds to the occupation of the room and incrementally distends or tightens the bulge in relation to body heat.

OPPOSITE, L TO R: 'Innerside', Katherine Clarke; photomontage, MWA; FROM ABOVE: Model views; 'Purity and Tolerance' at the Architecture Foundation

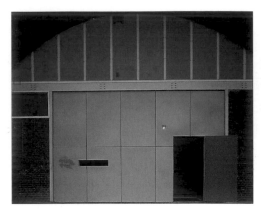
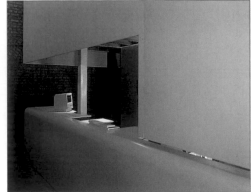

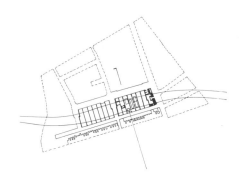

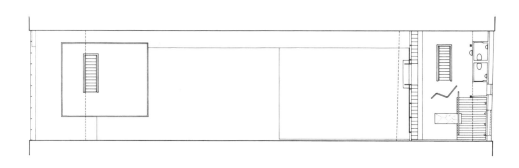

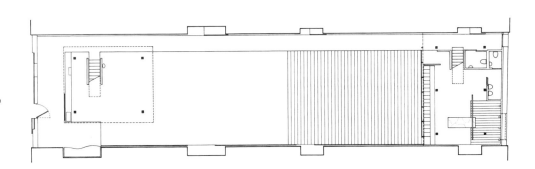

GYMNASIUM

Waterloo, London, UK

The gymnasium is a railway arch spanning two streets under Waterloo East Station. Into this single volume are inserted two independent steel-frame structures. One appears as a figure reflected in the mirror which conceals the other. The first is a wrapped steel platform holding cardiovascular equipment, the second, concealed behind the wall of mirror, houses the changing rooms.

There is an intentional discretion in the successive wrapping and revealing of the steel frame and the arch by the sheet materials of pale stove-enamelled steel, plywood, laminates, Portuguese marble and mirror, which are in turn on occasion lined with colour. This modesty of disclosure is repeated in the passage from the street as a series of glimpses and sliced views which end in the women's changing room, from where the viewer can survey the entire volume unseen.

ABOVE LEFT: Site location plan; RIGHT, FROM ABOVE: Second floor plan; first floor plan; longitudinal section

UNITED KINGDOM

MATTHEW PRIESTMAN ARCHITECTS

After working with Chris Wilkinson, then as project architect for a high-rise industrial project in Hong Kong, and for Canary Wharf Building FC-3 (with Troughton McAslan), and briefly, with Will Alsop, Matthew Priestman set out, rationally or rashly, during this apparently unending cultural/economic recession, to form his own practice.

Being the only means for a studio to work beyond the constraints of smaller projects and the all-consuming pragmatism essential for survival, competition entries began. With a second prize for the Waverley competition, first prize and commission for a Leonard Cheshire Home project, AJ Bovis award in 1993, and first prizes for the Bangour Masterplan (with Kinnear Landscape Architects and Duncan Berntsen) and the Ørestad Masterplan competitions (with Andrew Yeoman, Paul Pindelski and John Cramer), amongst other results, media exposure followed.

Current work includes private houses, in particular a 300-square-metre new-build project in Herefordshire; a 26-unit low-cost housing scheme in Scotland; a complex mixed-use and retail redevelopment in London; and seven stations for the Copenhagen Minimetro, a new £350 million partially underground light rail system serving and funded by the Ørestad site, in collaboration with Henning Larsens Tegnestue. Working with Ted Happold, David Watkins (sculptor), and Andy Anderson on the National Museum of Korea and Prado Redevelopment competitions proved to be highly productive and expansive.

Projects have loosely employed the analogy of 'organism', be it sociological, zoological or botanical; internal activity between parts and components is seamlessly combined with external and environmental relations, producing an active complexity in the parallels and/or overlaying of function, device or relationship.

Neural nets, structuralist 'structures', the modern city, the solar system, and so on form references – scale and definition is an arbitrary selection – such that working on a masterplan or a piece of furniture is equally desirable and possible.

The process and product of the work are intended to be assimilative: apposite clarity is not perceived as reductive, but rather as the resultant of a more symbiotic and consensus-like tendency.

This open-ended stance allows differing approaches, as the circumstance and character of each project suggests.

Proposals for the University College of South Stockholm, combining large-scale strategies with a regenerative impetus, draws upon the Chinese (medicine) image of the 'human body as landscape'; the project is preoccupied with the interaction of parts and external connections.

The National Museum of Korea project derives its building form from six groups of metaphor, whilst the Prado project is concerned with reconnecting a matrix of existing buildings, the tectonic overlap of upper and lower principal floors and translucency in between.

God's in the soup – as well as the detail.

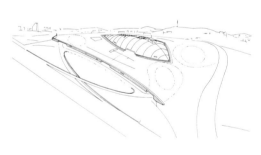

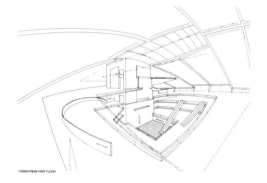

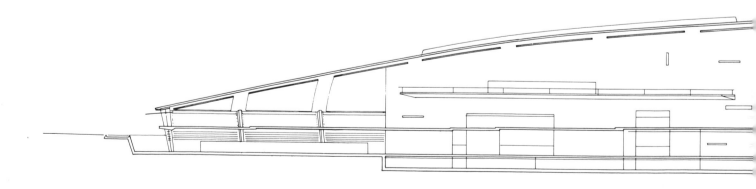

ABOVE, L TO R: Aerial perspective; sketch; tower from first floor; BELOW: Section

NATIONAL MUSEUM OF KOREA

Seoul, Korea

*An international competition requested pro-
posals for a new museum to be placed in a
mature park near central Seoul. This project
submission was completed in collaboration
with Ted Happold (sadly now deceased), Büro
Happold Consulting Engineers, David Watkins
and Andy Anderson.*

*Centrally planned around an open well, the
building is served by an underground rail
station and parking, so that only pedestrian
access at park level is visible.*

*The building elements are distinct and
interact: well, wall, tower, platforms, shell,
moat and landscape.*

*The burial mound-like triangulated shell
form, in timber lattice shell construction with
a stainless steel skin, is intended to draw upon
Korean culture. The presentation of the proposal gives outlines of six groups of references, and in combining these together, an
enigmatic redolence is intended:*

> *Eye: universal and emphatic organ of sight;*
> *Chrysalis: emblem of transformation and
> emergence, with protective and sensitive
> skin;*
> *Earth: gravitas and the idea of a cyclical
> medium of nourishment and decay;*
> *Well: a physical excavation of the earth, the
> source of life-giving water;*
> *Strata: geological and historical – sequen-
> tial and hierarchical order;*
> *Yin/Yang: holistic combination of opposites
> – the juxtaposition of ideas.*

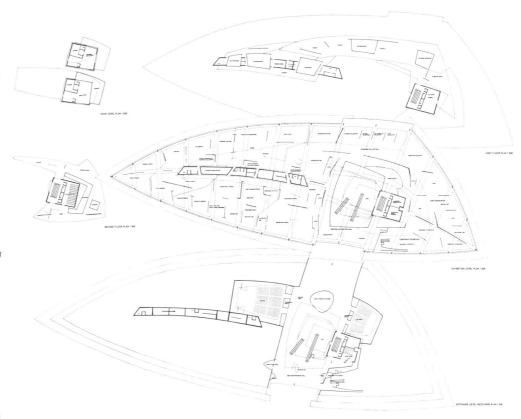

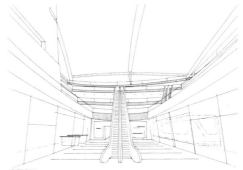

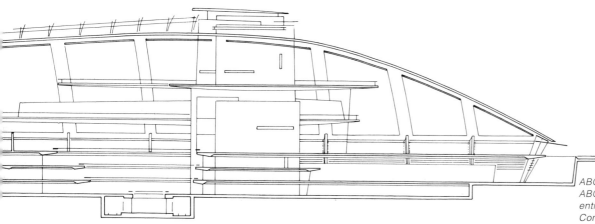

*ABOVE LEFT: Roof level plan; second floor plan;
ABOVE RIGHT: First floor plan; exhibition level plan;
entrance level mezzanine plan; CENTRE, L TO R:
Concept model; view from station; strata*

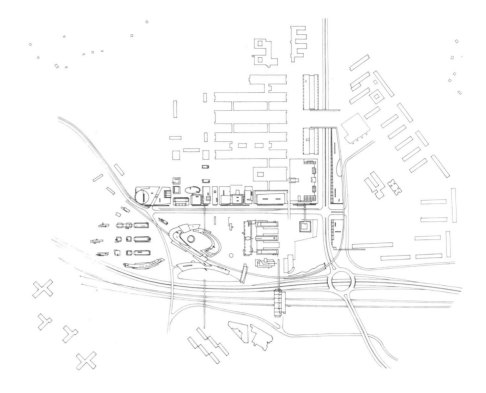

*FROM ABOVE, L TO R: Model detail views; site plan;
cross-section; model; section through libraries*

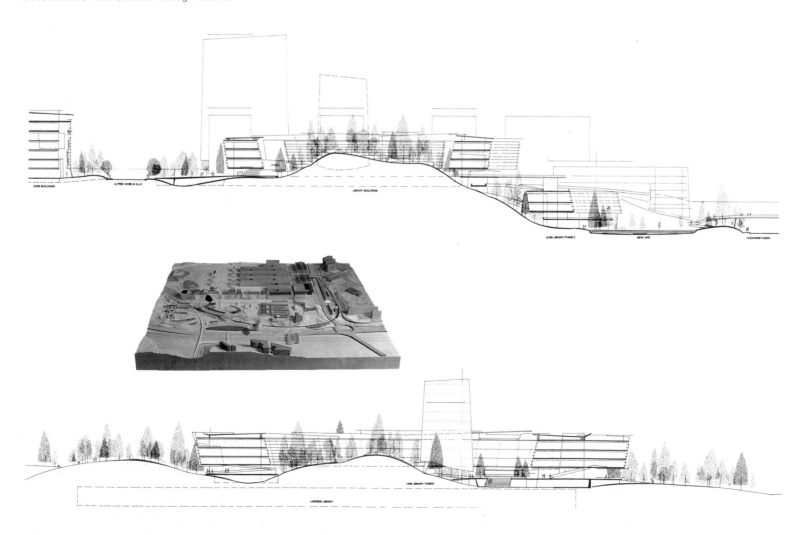

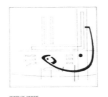

The Body As Garden

BODY OF PARTS

HEART AND MIND

ENCLOSURE

CONNECTION

UNIVERSITY COLLEGE OF SOUTH STOCKHOLM

Stockholm, Sweden

This proposal has been developed for an open two-stage competition for a 325,000-square-metre teaching and research campus, to be assembled around existing hospital and residential areas, within an undulating, wooded landscape. Matthew Priestman Architects, and four Swedish practices, have been commissioned to submit final proposals in July 1996.

The purpose of providing facilities is combined with the objective of implanting generative activity into a depressed suburban district.

A gradation of density, scale and activity is seen as essential, and four organising ideas are used:

Body of parts – concepts and components are intended to interact, and the analogy of a living body is identified, with organs, nerves and flesh;

Heart and mind – intelligent centre;

Enclosure – degrees of enclosure and openness, privacy and sharing;

Connections – the important rail infrastructure and new curving cycle/footpath forms a network of internal and external connections.

With Andy Anderson, Isabel Giesler, Rachel O'Borne and Jessie Marshall. Model by A Models, London.

FROM ABOVE, L TO R: 'The body as garden'; the four elements and site; model; section through Halsovagen; model; section through Alfred Nobels Alle

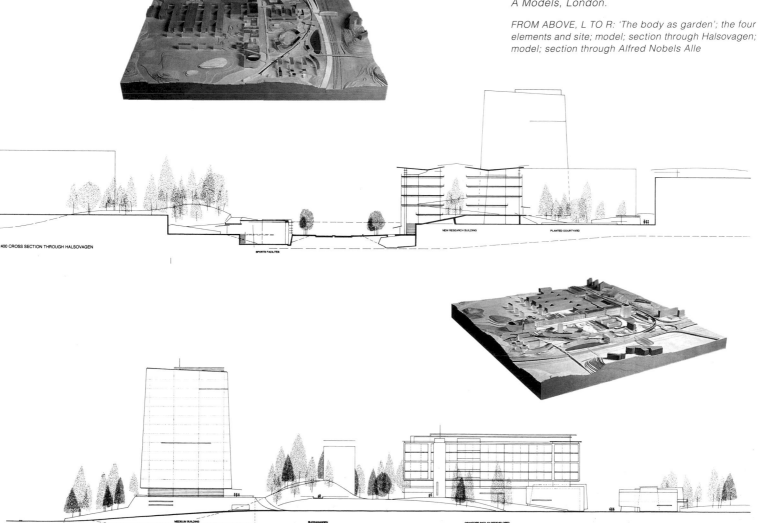

1:400 CROSS SECTION THROUGH HALSOVAGEN

1:400 SECTION THROUGH ALFRED NOBELS ALLE

UNITED STATES OF AMERICA

DALY, GENIK

Material Works

The relationship of materials to the process of construction is an essential point of departure for our work; we emphasise the development of a material vocabulary guided by intuition, research and expertise. The inherent qualities of materials are the aspects of design that unify the effort of the workshop and the product of the factory. In our work we look for similarities between materials in addition to contrast. We search for their possible transformations, through the process of manufacture, refinement and wear.

In recent projects we have been examining the interface between conventions of construction and customised fabrication. The construction of these conflicting and complementary processes can be the basis for critical organisation and architectural logic.

SALZMAN RESIDENCE

Tarzana, California

A 1968 tract house was demolished to its perimeter walls. New living spaces cluster around large cabinet and screen elements. A fireplace clad in aluminium serves to define one edge of the new living room. Light from a new clerestory above is reflected off the fireplace's wrinkled skin. A wooden pivoting screen of stressed skin spruce enables the dining room to close up for intimate dinners or open for large gatherings.

In the garden a galvanised steel canopy protects the family room from the glare of the sun while providing a setting for outdoor meals.

BELOW: Plan; OPPOSITE, FROM ABOVE: Composite drawing of architectural components; sections

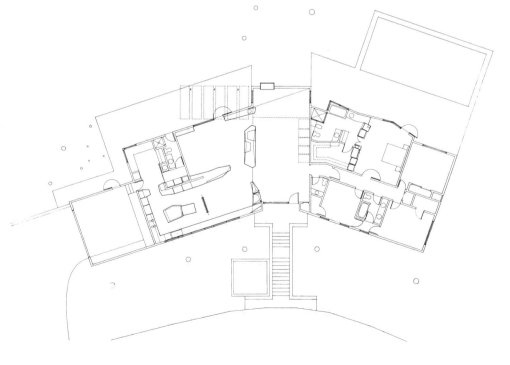

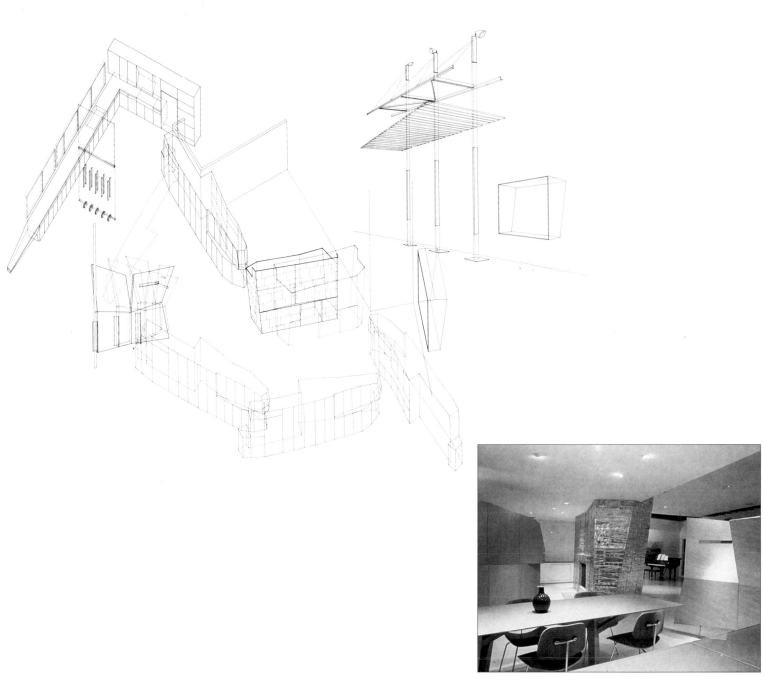

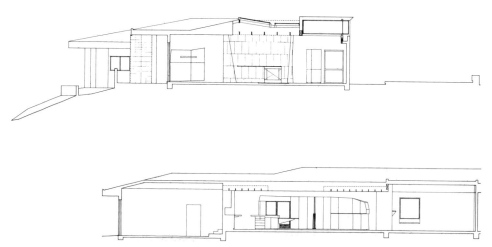

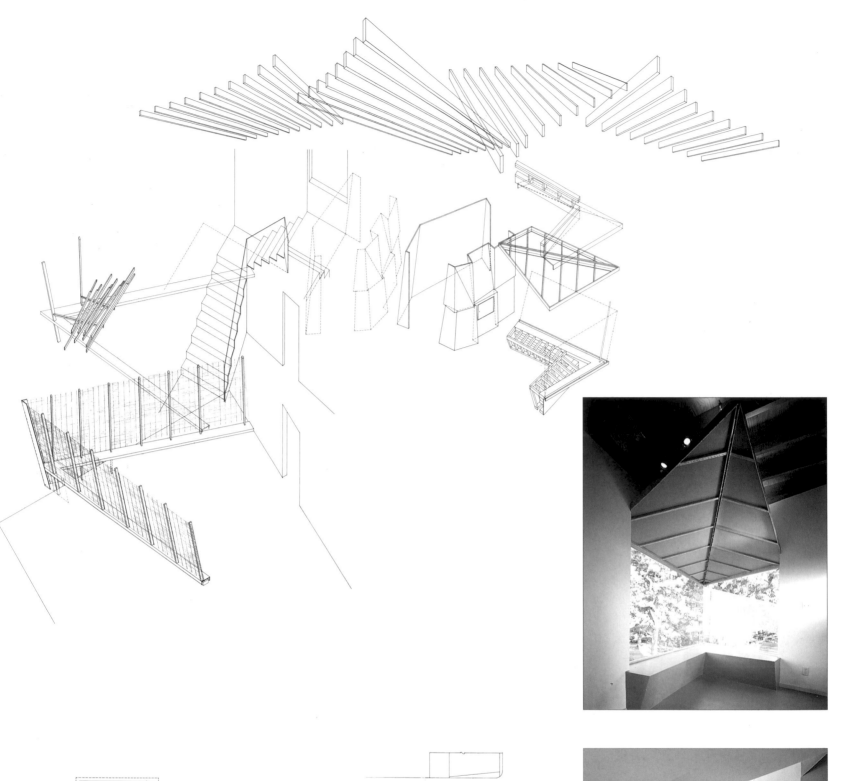

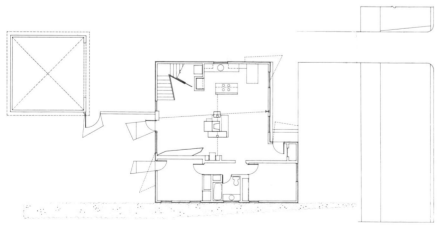

90

MOOSER-AVAKIAN RESIDENCE

Santa Monica, California

A simple sleeping loft with a large cantilevered viewing window is positioned on a terrace that replaces an existing gabled roof.

The old lower storey and the new upper storey are joined by a steel moment frame which braces the structure and bears the load of the new construction. New indoor and outdoor rooms are fashioned to form a progression from living spaces to sleeping spaces.

BELOW: Section; upper level plan; OPPOSITE, FROM ABOVE: Composite drawing of architectural components; lower level plan

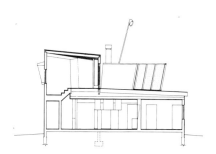

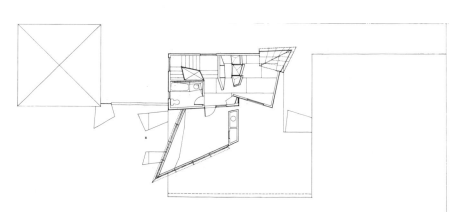

UNITED STATES OF AMERICA

GUTHRIE + BURESH

**A Conditional Manifesto:
Reading-in-Reverse**

*It is never dark and there are no stars in
Los Angeles.*

– Los Angeles
An uninterrupted blue-on-blue horizon
under a dominant sky.

– Continuing work
Schindler, Eames and Gehry. Smithson,
Irwin and Heizer.

– 1988-96
Politically and socially charged yet eco-
nomically chilled. Mud slides, riots, brush
fires and earthquakes.

– Incremental process
Autonomous partial projects focused on
particular concerns subsequently syn-
thesised.

– SiteWork
Tools for seeing, observation and docu-
mentation. Recording observed difference to make difference. Difference in
the movement of the sun. Difference in
the fall of the ground. Difference in the
position, massing and use of neighbouring buildings.

– FormWork
Reductive formal vocabulary challenged
through perceptually complex use of
space and materials. An irreducible
joining of structure and membrane, form
and space.

– Fictions
Conventional programme *in absentia* and
a post-scripting in three ways: mytho-
poetic descriptive habitation; hybridised
programmatic invention; optical breach or
transgression between spaces of normative isolation.

– Seamlessness
A blurring of distinctions between infrastructure and object, landscape and
building, private and public.

– Material character
Opacity: shadow and absorption.
Isolation and difference.
Transparency: light and reflection.
Same-ness and narcissism.
Translucent: diffuse and blurred. Spatial
boundary or extension in a state of con-
tinuous flux dependent upon the condi-
tion of the light and the position of the
observer.

– City buildings: Building cities
Relevant urban composition involving
value laden deployment of programme,
position and form.

Danelle Guthrie and Tom Buresh are
architects. They practise in Los Angeles
and teach at SCI-Arc.

POETIC JUSTICE

Hollywood, California

In association with Edwin Chan

*Located in a two-storey warehouse at the
western edge of Hollywood are the offices and
studios of Poetic Justice, an advertising and
associated creative arts concern with a client
base in the film industry. The project was
initiated by a series of conversations with the
client which focused on his desire for physical
isolation and psychological empowerment,
combined with the dynamic occupation of the
spaces made necessary by the unforeseeable
day-to-day fluctuations of the work. This
dynamic quality is expressed literally through
movable partitions constructed of a number
of materials: glass, transparent and translucent; medium-density fibreboard and painted
plaster board. Spatially articulated through
the nature of their motion, these partitions
slide, rotate and pinwheel past and around
each other to unfold a number of perceptual
spatial permutations. Like an optical labyrinth,
each spatial reading is juxtaposed with per-
petually changing transparency, conjuring not
one but multiple possibilities in its perceptual
orientation.*

OPPOSITE ABOVE: Alternative plan configurations

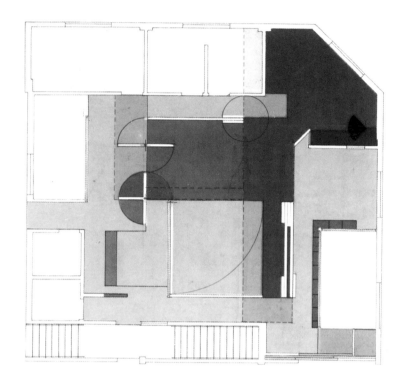

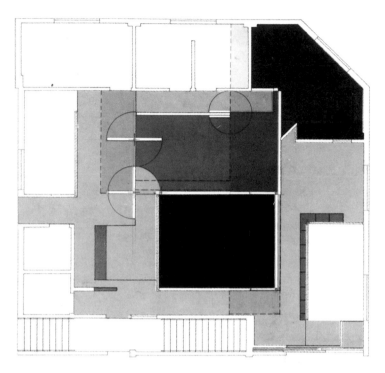

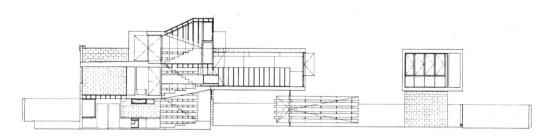

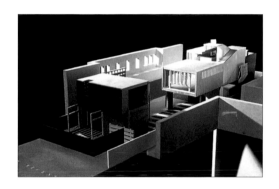

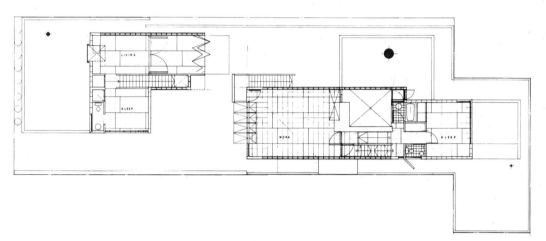

WORK/HOUSE

West Hollywood, California

Accessed by a commuter boulevard, the project provides two affordable WorkHouses. The street unit, positioned to form a physical and aural buffer to the rest of the site, consists of a ground floor studio and covered parking space, an upper floor living space and exterior deck. The garden unit, which will be occupied as both studio and living space, contains joined interior and exterior living space and a two-bay parking area on the ground level, and a studio, two bedrooms and two bathrooms on the upper levels. Interior spaces are designed more as extensions to adjacent exterior space than as programmatic containers.

Overlapping intermediate spaces between the two units as well as between the units and neighbouring properties, allow for a shared visual space (a suburban piazza) beyond the boundary of property walls. Materials are deployed for their experiential characteristics; their ability both to contribute to the multiple spatial understandings and to breach normative public/private distinctions. The WorkHouse employs the changing perception of enclosure as the primary component in a flexural composition.

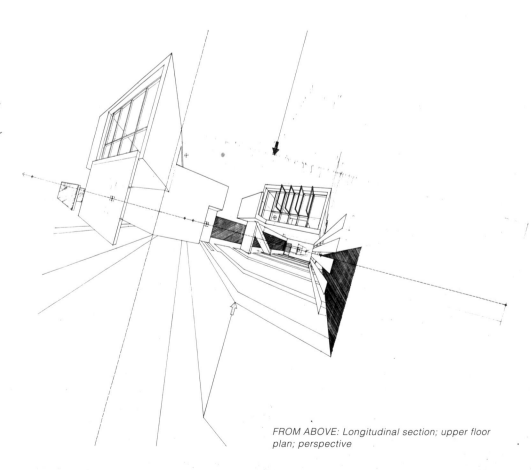

FROM ABOVE: Longitudinal section; upper floor plan; perspective

95

... WHY BECOME AN ARCHITECT?

Pity the poor architect, as he or she strives to make a living and to keep the art of architecture alive in the face of an ever more demanding clientele which is bent on getting better buildings for less money. Add to this the burden of increasingly closer statutory regulation aimed at making the architect responsible for the long-term performance of buildings and their impact on the public and the environment, and the disincentives to architectural practice become even clearer. Neither is architecture an easy route to affluence. Architect's earnings are poor in comparison with those of other professionals.

Kenneth Powell

... the changing role of architects means that they might be less involved with the 'technology of construction', but they must be involved with the 'construction of technology' instead. They have to be instrumental in the construction of the new computerised technologies that are already transforming building and design processes ... The design of new conditions for architecture of course means new attitudes towards the activities that take place in the architectural spaces they design: a new attitude towards programmes and the production of events, so as to reconfigure and provide a rich texture of experiences that will redefine architecture and urban life. The challenge is enormously exciting.

Bernard Tschumi

Nowadays the system is so doctrinaire that it's very hard for anyone with talent to survive. By the time students have been brainwashed for five years in an architectural school, by the time they have gone in for various awards and found that the gold medals are only given to the good boys, they will have given up the pursuit of excellence.

Quinlan Terry

How can architects base their architecture on prediction and control any longer? When will they learn to be mobile, spontaneous, expansive in their engagement with the world? It will be increasingly difficult for architects who believe that this is becoming the only acceptable condition for making architecture, for architects who believe that architecture represents the eternal verities, something of the human that is more universal and timeless than the messy and ephemeral events of the present ...

Lebbeus Woods

My definition of the profession is entirely in terms of its knowledge base and its ownership and extension in various ways, not least by an educational programme which transmits it from one generation to another. In architecture we have a particular kind of knowledge which is extremely interesting because it withers outside the context of action. Design, which means inventing the future not just for ourselves but for the people for whom we work, is the essence of the kind of knowledge that architecture represents. This can not be developed in the world of commerce or the universities alone but through architecture in practices – in the way architecture is delivered.

Francis Duffy

When I was asked what I wanted to do, I used to say 'be an opera singer'. My brothers wanted me to become an astronaut. They thought I would not make it in architecture as it was a waste of time. Many years ago when I won a competition I received a fax saying 'Mission Accomplished'.

Zaha Hadid